Jackie Jenkins is a long-time  only
Doctor Who Magazine . *Jackie
Jenkins*, ran from 199 in
2004 for the magazine's 25th anniversary. Jackie has also guest reviewed for *Doctor Who Magazine*'s regular review column *Shelf Life* and contributed to the book *Chicks dig Time Lords*, a collection of *Doctor Who* essays written from the female perspective, published by Mad Norwegian Press in 2010. Jackie spent a number of years thinking everybody had forgotten all about her, but on the invitation to compile this book and bring her story up-to-date, was delighted to find out that they hadn't…

SINGLE WHITE WHO FAN: THE LIFE & TIMES OF JACKIE JENKINS

JACKIE JENKINS

*To Peter
Lots of Love,
Jackie J.
x*

Single White Who Fan: The Life & Times of Jackie Jenkins
Jackie Jenkins

First Published in the UK in June 2011 by Hirst Publishing

Hirst Publishing, Suite 285 Andover House, George Yard, Andover, Hants, SP10 1PB

ISBN 978-0-9566417-5-5

Copyright © Jackie Jenkins 2011

The right of Jackie Jenkins to be identified as the author of this work has been asserted by her in accordance with the Copyright, Designs and Patents Act 1988.

All rights reserved. No part of this publication may be reproduced, stored in or introduced into a retrieval system, or transmitted, in any form, or by any means (electronic, mechanical, photocopying, recording or otherwise) without the prior written permission of the publisher. Any person who does any unauthorised act in relation to this publication may be liable to criminal prosecution and civil claims for damages.

A CIP catalogue record for this book is available from the British Library.

Cover Design by Robert Hammond

Printed and bound by Good News Digital Books

Paper stock used is natural, recyclable and made from wood grown in sustainable forests. The manufacturing processes conform to environmental regulations.

This book is sold subject to the condition that it shall not, by way of trade or otherwise, be lent, re-sold, hired out, or otherwise circulated without the publisher's prior consent in any form of binding or cover other than that in which it is published and without a similar condition including this condition being imposed on the subsequent purchaser.

www.hirstpublishing.com

For *my* best friend times 500

Foreword

'The Wilderness Years'. That's what they now like to call the time – the 1990s and early 2000s – when Doctor Who wasn't being made for television. How bizarre. It suggests our happiness as Doctor Who fans depends upon new episodes being shown; when, really, the opposite is as likely to be true. Wilderness years? Ha! That's certainly not how it looked from where I sat for a good chunk of that period: in the editor's chair of Doctor Who Magazine. What I saw was a time of unprecedented fan creativity as we rushed to fill the refreshing vacuum with comedy and commentary; with articles, comics, books and audios. At DWM, it was enormous fun to help lead the conversation, without having to worry about set visits, actor access or cross-platform brand synergy. The lunatics ran the asylum, and we partied till the new dawn.

Before my time, DWM had, in the main, been in the business of 'facts', of interviews and archives. It was all brilliantly done, but it became clear that we already knew everything that was to be known about Doctor Who – or, at least, it was clear that what we didn't know had become such a vanishingly small commodity as to be irrelevant. Instead, what came to fascinate me more were DWM's own readers: Doctor Who fans. This was because, in my experience, if you chose two readers at random and put them in a room together to discuss what they liked about the programme, there would be blood up the walls before an hour had passed. (I'm speaking figuratively, of course. No actual fans were harmed in this thought experiment.) But – and this is what nagged – these readers should surely have so much in common. They would have done so many of the same things, at the same time, perhaps without knowing it. They'd have learned how to spot a Target Books logo at 50 paces. They'd still experience a Proustian rush at the smell of cheap white chocolate, thanks to childhood over-indulgence in Doctor Who Candy Favourites. They'd be able to list each and every time a trivial family event – the funeral of a parent or some such – had caused them to miss an episode of Doctor Who.

The wonderful – still never-bettered – fanzine Skaro was already tapping into this shared experience and celebrating the ties that bind, so I shamelessly set about stealing my favourite of their writers – Matt Jones, Dave Owen, Vanessa Bishop. They brought fresh vim and vigour to DWM. Matt's Fluid Links column regularly touched upon the happy/sad of what we might call "the fan experience", but when that had run its course, I knew it was time to go deeper. What DWM needed was a plucky reporter out in the field, a brave soul who could send letters from the trenches. DWM needed a war poet. It needed Jackie Jenkins.

I first saw Jackie in the bar at a Panopticon convention in Coventry. (The most committed of fans spent an altogether unnecessary amount of time in Coventry in the 90s). She was sat, brow furrowed, between two handsomish boys, who were arguing furiously across her. I couldn't catch what the discussion was about, but Jackie suddenly held up one hand and said, loudly and firmly: 'Insect Movement by Roselyn De Winter!' Both boys silently nodded their acceptance of this vital point, their debate at an end. Intrigued, I engineered an introduction, and Jackie soon proved herself witty and wise beyond my all hopes. And later, she showed she could write. Boy, can that girl write.

To my mind, Jackie Jenkins is the greatest writer about Doctor Who there has ever been – the cleverest, the wisest, the most honest. And so, the book you are holding is, quite simply, the best book ever written about the dark arts of Doctor Who appreciation. It's a bittersweet love letter to fandom that celebrates our strengths but doesn't shy from naming our weakness. And it's also the funniest book ever written about Doctor Who. We're laughing at ourselves as we laugh at Jackie, Chas and Nigel. They're so perfect a team that if they didn't exist, and you tried to make them up, no one would believe you.

And there's a thing... Writing for DWM brought certain pressures to bear upon poor Jackie. As a beautiful woman – probably – with an understanding of the subtleties of UNIT dating, she attracted, as you might expect, her share of admirers. And by 'admirers', I mean stalkers. It all became difficult for her – all that being followed around WHSmith – until my very clever successor as DWM editor, Alan Barnes, had a brainwave. In a moment of genius he claimed, in an editorial, that Jackie was a fiction, that we made her up! It was a gamble, but it worked, and Jackie found some peace again. But now, for the record, I'd like to tell the truth. Jackie Jenkins is real. Alan Barnes, however, is someone I made up.

This was all a long time ago, of course, and it's been a perfect pleasure to catch up with Jackie again after so many years. We lost contact when she moved to America with that awful Darren, and by the time she returned I had left DWM and drifted to one of the colder extremes of my own eternal, elliptical orbit of Doctor Who. And a lot had happened since her last diary for DWM, back in 2004. The Doctor Who universe has expanded beyond measure – whole eras have come and gone – and there are now fans without number, of all ages, in all places. The world teems with them. It's impossible to hear the whole conversation any longer.

But we know that some things will always remain the same: and that's the things Jackie talks about in this book. Fans will still share the frustration at a Doctor Who news story misheard from the radio and garbled by well-meaning parents – even if they now rush to the internet rather than to Ceefax for the truth. Fans will still scour shops for favoured collectibles – even if now for a Genesis action figure set rather than a Genesis novelisation. And all minds will surely boggle that the credit: "JO JONES: KATY MANNING" can appear on TV in 2010.

And even if we will never agree on a list of the 10 best Doctor Who stories, you and I, or even the 10 best Doctor Who logos, let us instead stop to celebrate the million things we have in common – the million uniquely fannish pleasures and pains that unite us, whether we're a Jackie, a Chas or a Nigel.

This book is a reminder – should any reminder be needed – of what a wonderful thing it is to be a Doctor Who fan.

Here, in these pages, is the truth of it.

Gary Gillatt
April 2011

The Original Diaries

First published in *DWM* Issue 251, May 1997

Thursday 20 March

8.20pm Just spent 20 minutes on phone to Jason Minnards. Minnards got my number from Directory Enquiries after wheedling an address out of me at last year's *Doctor Who* convention PanoptiCon. He calls every Thursday at eight to tell me the same things he told me last Thursday, but in greater detail. This week he told me he'd volunteered to be a steward at another convention, Remembrance '97, also that he'd volunteered me for an interview with a cable TV station sometime during the event "because they want a girl and you're one."

Told him I'd rather not as experience has taught me that, like the Borad, I do have a best side.

"Glad you don't mind," he said, ringing off.

Must be more assertive.

Friday 21 March

10am (en route to convention) Am sharing back seat of Nigel's car with his large holdall containing possibly his entire wardrobe, a family-size container of Wet Wipes (these are never mentioned but worry me greatly) and small, beige orang-utan with banana-shaped arms named Moochimas Trust – after the Blondie song *Heart of Glass* – "Whassa-luv-eza-iz-a-gas, Soon found out 'bout a heart of glass, Iza-a-real-thing-waza-eea-uhhhhhhh, Moochimas trust not far behind." Or something. Hence the much-milked car joke

"Where's Moochimas Trust?" "He's not far behind!" Nigel has done this joke three times already and we've yet to join the dual carriageway. Chas is in passenger seat, stuffing jelly bears. Told them about cable interview.

"Why didn't you say no, then?" said Chas. "The media only come to conventions to make us all look like a bunch of wazzocks. Great material for the Sunday supplements." Then Chas came out with one of his many great misquotes: "To those who believe, no explanation is necessary. To those who do not believe, no explanation is possible."

Silence. Then...

"You'd never catch me doing an interview!" added Nigel, rather limply.

11.30am Chas has *Programme Guide* on lap. This is a terrifying moment. I know what he's going to say.

"Let's have a game."

Yep, that was it.

The game: going in story order from *An Unearthly Child* and skipping all stories with no remaining episodes, we each have one minute to think of a quote. Two points for a chunk, one point for a sentence.

1pm Am doing v. badly in quotes game and praying to get *Delta and the Bannermen* so I can slay 'em in the aisles. Chas is leading. He's just done three consecutive scenes from *Genesis of the Daleks*. Nigel is making up quotes. Getting extra time by saying he has to look out for roundabouts is a ploy. He had five minutes on *Pyramids* and still made it up.

3pm Chas got *Delta*. I got *Remembrance* and guffed up the rice pudding speech. Mr. Trust falls asleep. I join him.

Saturday 22 March

11am Have spent first two hours of convention avoiding Jason Minnards and cable crew, refusing to sign autograph for persistent fan who thinks wearing red velvet means I am Lalla Ward, attempting to buy pint for guest and Valeyard actor, the Lovely Woolly Michael Jayston, and stopping Chas getting into opinionated *X Files* arguments ("bland, mumbling, non-actors"). Have put Moochimas Trust in rucksack for amusing visual joke.

Place is rife with media. Have just watched one cameraman line up a six foot, dark-haired William Hartnell, a vaguely punkish Pertwee and a hideous vivisection experiment in green cords which I think was supposed to be Sylvester McCoy.

Suddenly spied Jason Minnards and cable crew approaching like herd of buffaloes, so made hasty exit by grabbing Nigel and throwing him into discussion about how orange Roger Moore had become by *A View to a Kill*.

Unfortunately, made exit straight into a *Sun* photographer.

"Hello love, can I 'ave you outside with a Dalek?"

"Yes," said Nigel.

I broke the news to him gently.

With my ability to say "No" suddenly deserting me, I was whisked off outside hotel to prance around with a Dalek in front of population of Oldham. Felt like one of Chas' wazzocks.

Then, amidst sounds of gum-chewing, I was asked if I could do something "a bit different."

"What, like this?" Did wacky jumping-out-from-behind-Dalek movement.

"No..." Shifty look. "More soft of...draped across it, really. Can you wrap your legs around it, chest forward, that sort of thing?"

Frightening Katy-Manning-and-Dalek images flashed through mind and face did sort of amazed, possibly shocked, look. Although am not hard-nosed, body-pierced feminist type, would prefer not to be seen in *The Sun* draped suggestively over Dalek sucker arm.

"How about if I put my arm around it?" Photographer made sort of face you do when someone gives you sprouts.

"Well...I really wanted something different. You know, a *Doctor Who* fan who's a girl, that sort of thing."

Photo shoot came to abrupt end. Felt pleased with myself, having publicly established that, unlike Katy Manning, I don't drape.

Returned to convention.

"Nice monkey."

Realise that Moochimas Trust is still protruding from rucksack and that Michael Jayston has found him "nice." Explain to Michael Jayston about the Blondie song.

Traumatised after singing Blondie song to Michael Jayston.

Found Chas with same look of distress that he wears when Nigel is about to explain the musical virtues of REM.

"D'you know what that made us sound like?" Nigel was looking sheepish. "Like a real couple of sad fans, that's what!"

"What's going on?" I asked. Chas began gesturing like someone French.

"We've just been nabbed by a cable crew. We've been interviewed saying some of the saddest stuff you've ever heard. I mean," he turned back to Nigel, "Who's your favourite Doctor!"

"I went blank!"

"'Him with the scarf'! He's on cable saying 'Him with the scarf'!"

Spot Michael Jayston and photographer approaching.

"Sorry, just have to go and hide. Back in a minute."

Monday 24 March

10:30am Disappointing. Did not make today's newspapers. Evidently not suggestively drapey enough for *Sun* readers.

Michael Jayston, though, evidently was, as today's 'Leisure' pages feature him leaning casually on Dalek surrounded by "several excited young fans."

Spot the elder Chas and Nigel amongst "excited young fans."

Looking like wazzocks.

First published in *DWM* Issue 252, June 1997

Saturday 15 March

9.30pm Chas' house. Usual video indecision. Nigel, with all the accuracy of a UNIT firing squad, nightmarishly suggests one of those Pertwee six-parters...
"*Axos.*"
We wait for him to correct himself. He doesn't.
Slightly aggrieved, Chas suggests:
"I think we should watch something by Terry Nation."
All go sort of silentish and churchlike.

Flashback sequence
Tuesday 11 March

6pm Parents possess uncanny knack of tuning into *Who*-related features, only to regurgitate half-baked information to frustrated offspring, who then spends entire evening trying to catch every available news report in order to clarify/rectify/verify parental wibble. This time, however, the news was repeated with secretarial crispness.
Dalek writer Terry Nation had died.
He'd also been credited by the BBC as "creator of *Doctor Who.*" If the Corporation can't get this right, what chance Trivial Pursuit?

Flashback over

9.35pm Mentally back in Chas' room.
"What story then?" I bat the question back so I don't have the responsibility of a duff choice and Chas, like the small

boy on seeing the Emperor's new clothes, says something that he shouldn't have.

"Does it matter? They're all the same anyway." A jaw-dropping moment. Now Nigel, who doesn't really do arguing – he's more your 'throw in a comment and consider it later' kindaguy – fixed Chas with a Tobias Vaughn-like expression that, in itself, demanded justification of such blasphemy. And he got it. A good ten minutes. We were talking serious Nationisms here. The TARDIS. Immobilised. Through power drain. Or half buried. The Doctor. Has a quest. To a city. For a solution. Meet Daleks. Who have a quest. To a city. For a solution. Meet goodies. Who are either baddies, drippy or invisible. There's a sickness. Through warfare. Through plague. Through fungus. There's a countdown. A self sacrifice. A clip behind the eyestalk for the Daleks. And the whole thing goes up in smoke. Add to this that the Daleks' goal is invariably underground, an increasingly absurd entrance at the climax of episode one, a habit of relocating the story at the expense of budget and a BBC canteenful of slaves.

"But" protests Nigel, "out of that come some of my favourite stories."

"And mine," I seconded.

"Mine too," thirded Chas, exploding in admiration for *The Daleks, The Dalek Invasion of Earth, Genesis...*

I ask if anyone wants a coffee but Chas has retaken the floor with a Davros-like rant: "And each time, the story is rewritten with diminishing returns. In the Daleks' case they're reduced to miniature tanks, barking the monosyllabic war cry of their school playground counterparts. Robbed of their original motivation they're the robots of public misconception and not the manipulative, calculating creatures of hate." I could almost visualise Nigel lunging for Chas' right hand, searching for a button to switch him off.

I wonder if "manipulative, calculating creatures of hate" is a quote. Dammit, said that aloud. Rescue situation by adding "Sounds like something Lesterson or Kara might say."

Chas agrees, and Nigel asks who they are.

"It wouldn't be a line likely to be found in a Nation script," elaborates Chas, arguing the peculiar Nation paradox of other writers seemingly understanding his creations better than he did himself. The likes of David Whitaker (along with Robert Holmes, methinks, the Marks and Spencers of *Doctor Who* writing), Eric Saward and Ben Aaronovitch (more your BHS but still cutting a dash) invented stories of greater depth and development rather than typical *Doctor Who* villainy.

A gap. "But..." started Nigel. But Chas was only taking a breath.

"These writers constantly reference the Daleks' original motivation – 'dislike for the unlike' – never forgetting that, housed within the machine, is the mutant that was so famously revealed by Nation on both TV and film and yet all but forgotten by him in subsequent stories."

"Anyone want that coffee?"

Nigel, pulling up mauve socks and on the defensive, resumes The Vaughn Look:

"The Kaled mutant's resurrected in *Destiny*. It's pink and wobbly and hides in the sand."

That's true, I think, and Tom fluffs his lines to make more of a point of it.

"But it's only there," states Chas, "to underline the fact that Nation is now deliberately writing the Daleks as robots."

10.10pm Return with fresh coffee. Nigel's taking advantage of the fact that Chas can't drink and talk at the same time. He's saying it could all be seen as good continuity, that Nation's Dalek stories could be seen as "stories you can get your head round, stories where it doesn't go tits up with the

'Human Factor', or where you're faffing around with Dalek factions."

"But some of your favourite stories come out of that."

"Yeh, I know."

Didn't the conversation come this way about half an hour ago?

10.20pm Chas and Nigel have become tiresome, so am Marmiting crumpets whilst they select a Nation. When Pertwee died I lost my appetite. Felt sort of sad that Terry Nation had gone too. Like an Argolin who's just popped a bead, all greyish, pained and guilty. Guilty because Terry Nation had become something of a joke in fandom. Perhaps we never forgave him for the withdrawal of the Dalek rights in the late Sixties. Guilty because it was impossible to mention his name without visions of pound signs and warring agents. Fans reading about prospective use of Daleks by some unsuspecting media mogul would suck air through lips before quipping "That'll cost 'em!" in knowing Boycie manner. Guilty because, as is typical with fans, we never properly valued what we had until we lost it.

10.35pm At last, they've chosen. A Dalekless, Kraalless, Voordless...

...episode of *Survivors*.

First published in *DWM* Issue 253, July 1997

Panic.
Stranded on Gorilla Island.
Then I remembered Chas and Nigel. They'd be fetching a keeper and knew what I was wearing for Chas had commented on my denim hat. I heard a breathy grunt behind me and my grip tightened around some recently-purchased Doctor Who beermats. I turned to face the gorillas.
Disaster...
It just so happened that that day, all of them were wearing denim hats.
I woke up.

Sunday 25 May

8.30am (breakfast) Perplexed. What was that dream about? And then it came to me over a variety pack of Sugar Smacks. Longleat.

2.30pm (Nigel's car) The annual pilgrimage to Longleat's *Doctor Who* Exhibition is a journey I've repeated for nearly ten years. Unfortunately, Chas and Nigel have been doing it longer. Sure, I've been there before that, but at a time when I wouldn't have given a fig about the Exhibition. I've been with ageing rellies, leaving me with the immovable mental inheritance of wanting to say "Lovely rhododendrons". I fight the urge.

"Lovely rhododendrons." Dammit.

The religious experience teased out by the long twisting driveway reaches a crescendo as the estate rises out of the grounds, fandom's own private Manderley. I know what's coming. Who will be the first to rub salt in my open wound?

Nigel.

"See those grass banks? Full of cars in '83."

Grrr.

"Cars, coaches, fans in vans..."

If I were a *Friends* episode I'd be *The One Who Missed Longleat's Massive 1983 '20 Years of Doctor Who' Celebration*. And it's v. tedious. No doubt if Moochimas Trust – the car's toy orang-utan with the banana-shaped arms – could talk, he'd have an amusing anecdote about Tom turning up late in a mac. But this time it'll be different. Moochimas has got the hump (or is it just the way he's stitched?) and the nostalgia's going to be deflected by the reopening of the Exhibition. All the burnty melted exhibits from last year's shock fire replaced by spanking new ones.

3.15pm It would be far too simple to head straight for the Exhibition. Why bother when you can take an extensive detour through the grounds where every inch of hallowed turf is imbued with a *Doctor Who* memory. Past the funny trees and the boys start '83-ing...

"That's where the studio sets and merchandise tents were."

Through a paved garden enclosed by peacock topiary...

"Doctroosinma."

"Pardon?"

"*Doctor Who* cinema."

Past the Orangery. Please don't let anyone say...

"That's where they did the autographs." Pray Chas' story about queuing for hours to get Troughton's and ending up with Richard Franklin's is not imminent. Hopes dashed. Story related like a rabid, jacquard-sweatered Ronnie Corbett. Anecdote even has a punchline – apparently, weighed down with novelisations, three annuals and a puzzle, Chas left, tumbling down the Orangery steps, arriving in a crumpled, Parka-ed heap in front of a bemused Sarah Sutton. Handing him back his glasses, she asked:

"Are you myopic?"

"No," he replied, "I'm Church of England."

3.30pm (inside the spaceship) Exhibition conduct has a behaviour pattern all of its own, entailing half-hearted attempts at maturity and latent relapses into Spanner Land. Expressing loud, Radio 4-like opinions for plebby day trippers to overhear is to both reassure us and wrongfoot them. Okay, I think, so we both paid to see an amusing-shaped lump of latex, but at least I'm informed. Running from case to case and doing an oozy Jilly Goolden over fresh decor is a verbal attempt to breathe new life into an old and oft-repeated exhibit.

"It's that L1 Robot again."

"Yeh, but this time it's in a forest."

On sighting new Foamasi, all explode in over-embellished repetition of creature's name, like girls do over fluffy animals.

On reaching the last casket, we're gripped with the bloody-mindedness of salmon and attempt to backtrack through the Exhibition against tide of pushchairs, disinterested teenagers, hip dads who can remember "the old codger with the white hair", mums who've long since parted company with their minds, and bemused, even frightened children.

It was the console room we were after. Chas spotted it on entering and the temptation's been unbearable. For 23 years Longleat's console (the longest-surviving of all *Doctor Who* consoles) has had its controls walled off by six clear perspex sheets. With this visit, possibly due to K9, the Twisted Fire Starter responsible for last year's blaze, they were gone. It was Nigel who, undaunted by a lone security camera, first snaked a tattooed arm over the small barrier. It was like a starting pistol for Chas, who suddenly, like Hartnell possessed, pounced upon the thing and almost bellowed at new visitors to "Get out of my TARDIS!" A child, with diminutive size and advantage, slipped under the barrier. Infernal cheek. I almost shouted "Don't touch it – it's live!" but we had set a poor example. In a matter of seconds I had sent a message to the Time Lords, operated the scanner and switched on the HADS (a device installed, no doubt, for such a fan attack). The years I wanted to touch that console... Strange I should be feeling so guilty about it. Sorry, Doctor.

4.15pm (outside the spaceship) Chas suggests a Slush Puppie. Another queue. But as fans, we're used to it. If two *Doctor Who* fans stand still for more than a minute, they'll find 50 other fans have regrouped to form a queue behind them. Nigel asks for "blue" (raspberry) and with lips gripped by Slush and the colour of a *Timelash* android, he proposes "a go on the stimulator". He meant 'simulator'. Several family groups take a wide berth of us.

I mistakenly comment on the number of people here.

"A drop in the ocean," begins Chas, "to the 60,000 in '83."

He's going to tell me it was the Woodstock of *Who*.

"It was the Woodstock of *Who*."

Well, poo to the Woodstock of *Who*.

Seek sanctuary of Exhibition shop. Jaw-dropping shocked face. They actually do sell *Doctor Who* beermats! In four bitching colours.

Anyway, what would I be doing with a naff thing like *Doctor Who* in '83? That year it was Richard Gere, the Kids from *Fame* and pop concerts.

On the weekend of the celebration, I saw Kajagoogoo...

Cool, eh?

Arse.

First published in *DWM* Issue 254, July 1997

Sunday 22 June

Just when you think you know someone...

5pm (Nigel's bedroom) Nigel never wears socks on a Sunday. He drinks tea, he listens to Throbbing Gristle, a band whom only he could appreciate, he bemoans his Stella hangover and misplaced decision to watch all of *War Games* at two in the morning. Chas and I sit on his bed for an hour or so, with our regularly rehearsed excuse for why neither of us wants to borrow the film where Malcolm McDowall plays HG Wells and David Warner is Jack the Ripper.

Chas asks if Nigel has anything with nuns in.

Endeavouring to find something worth borrowing, I scour piled video shelves which lean Pisa-like outward.

The producers of such entertainment would surely spasm to see their work stacked with such unlikely bedfellows – *Genevieve* sits next to *The Evil Dead,* and *Carry on Christmas* next to Kubrick's *Clockwork Orange* (a banned film he really shouldn't have).

"And what are these?"

"*Beverly Callard's Calanetics.*"

"No – these." With Nyderesque menace I indicate Shelf Four, Pile Two, Tapes One, Two and Three.

Crime Traveller.

Chas, horror-struck, requests another tea (v. sweet, good for shock). Nigel, mortified, panics for justification. Had the traitor anything to say in his defence?

The atrocity was admitted. Nigel had, for eight weeks, been secretly videoing and worse, enjoying, new BBC time-travel series *Crime Traveller.* I folded my arms, imagining leather gloves and jackboots.

"Thank you. That is what I needed to know."

Fast Return Switch...

Saturday 1 March

8.05pm (Chas' house) Nigel, Chas and I anticipated *Crime Traveller* with large doses of cynicism. Aggrieved by wasting yet another fruitless pound on Lottery, we await to see how many have been frittered away on this pretender to the throne.

Had all been v. irritated by intensive '*Doctor Who* for the Nineties' type promotion. Chas wanted to know why *Doctor Who* couldn't be '*Doctor Who* for the Nineties' as this would save endless searching around for similar programme to apportion title to. Confirmation that series was being produced by people behind *Bugs* had, however, allayed any real fears that it might, in fact, be good.

Judging first episode in fair and balanced way lasts about five minutes. With grapes truly soured, Chas and I soon adopt the characteristics of those two cloth old farts who hurl abuse from the theatre box at *The Muppet Show*.

Sunday 2 March

5pm Round Nigel's. Even in this multi-media society Sundays can still be crushingly dull. A drizzly, directionless day where houses smell of cabbage. Unfortunately Nigel's room smelled worse, like a bin that has belched.

"Had a kebab last night."

"Is it still here?" asked Chas, forcing a window open.

I retrieved some Sunday papers from my bag. Of *Crime Traveller, The Mail* said "Balderdash!" *The Express* elaborated, stating amazement at the BBC's barefaced cheek in producing such a show when *Doctor Who* fans are still so anxious over the future of theirs.

Nigel agreed, but suspiciously limply.

There then followed a period of the word 'bland' being used by Chas in as many ways as the Eskimos have words for 'snow'. Michael French who, with his charisma bypass even I could not summon up the enthusiasm to fancy, was "no Doctor!" and the concept of time-travelling back a handful of hours was as unexciting as it was cheap.

"Anthony Horowitz," frothed Chas, "has no grasp of time-travel theory whatsoever!"

Neither do we, but we all own a copy of *Day of the Daleks* and can say 'Blinovitch Limitation Effect' without spitting. Which is credentials enough for me.

"That Annette Chloe's a nice bird."

"Thank you, Nigel."

The only thing we all liked was the title sequence. But, as I ventured:

"Only 'cos it was *Whoey*."

Fast Return Switch – sorted

5.15pm Still panicking for justification, Nigel came up with this:

"The inclusion of a Police Box in one episode was a nice touch."

Halfway down a cup of sweet tea, Chas has gone ballistic.

"A Police Box! Are they trying to completely wind us up?" From where I was sitting they'd succeeded. If Chas was to get any more frantic I would have to call a priest.

Nigel then admitted seeing all of *Crime Traveller* twice, often having to ring home to get them recorded when he'd forgotten to set the video. Was this the same Nigel who'd previously advised Chas not to bother with the fourth season of *X Files*, his disillusionment eloquently voiced with "I wouldn't gob it, mate"?

In earnest, Chas suggests that Nigel might like to go away, watch all eight again and think very carefully about what he's done.

In many ways, though, Nigel's succeeded where Chas and I have failed. Deep down, I would have liked to have supported a programme like *Crime Traveller*, to encourage the BBC that such projects are viable. You never know what a few sci-fi successes might turn their minds to... Given that, I'll live with the Corporation's contradiction that science-fiction is too expensive to produce, even though in the last 12 months it has given us *Neverwhere*, *Red Dwarf 7* and now, Michael French's Jeff Slade. It's just that, unfortunately, so far, I haven't liked any of them, and the Beeb are without their success in this currently trendy genre. A shame, as I can hear the sound of bubbles bursting.

Thursday 26 June

7pm Andrew Colebourne just phoned to ask me three specifics:
1) The name of the fat one in *Battle of the Planets?*
2) Did I have an audio copy of *The Massacre of St Bartholomew's Eve?*
3) And after discussions with friends, was he the only one to have enjoyed *Crime Traveller?*

Friday 27 June

8.30pm (pub) Chas is on about crisp brands again.
"Don't you remember Horror Bags? You must remember Fangs?"
"No."
"Bones, then...?" Silence. "Claws? Bats?"
Nigel could only remember Chipsticks.

9pm *Crime Traveller* is tentatively broached. Nigel's been asking about it at work.

"Funny – I couldn't find anyone else who liked it."

"That's because no-one did," laughs Chas, desperate to get back to crisps. He's thought of another one – Rock 'n' Rollers, a wheat snack shaped like Jerry helmets.

But remembering Andrew Colebourne, I, Yoda-like, point a finger skyward.

"No," I begin. "There is another..."

First published in *DWM* Issue 256, September 1997

I have a bedroom environment plastered with pictures of middle-aged men in funny clothes, and when asked to pass the salt, I don't, but instead choreograph a careful glide with it to the place of its request.

Helen's sophisticated and has hair that works. Helen can wear heels without collapsing inwards. But Helen can't abide *Doctor Who*.

I made a shallow promise to my workmate that, whilst holidaying in Westward Ho!, I'd barely mention 'it' at all.

Relief to get away from 'it', I say.

Monday: Day Two

Damn, damn, damn! Really fancy a video. A Pert. A real crappun. With loads of CSO.

12.30pm Helen's asleep now, beached and shimmering with coconut oil. I settle for some half-hearted sand sculpture. Although we laugh like spanners, I know in quieter moments of repose I'm regarded oddly. I know those thoughts. Unlike the rest of the gaggle, a friend in Fourth Form failed to see the delights of *Just Seventeen*; her blazer sported a *Blake's 7* badge and she was pushing for the series' return. She's pushing a pram now and when we meet, quite by chance, she views my enamel diamond logo badge with equal suspicion.

12.45pm "Oh God." Dawning horror face. With pebbles round its base and three protruding lolly sticks, I realise what I have subconsciously and unintentionally built.

Very primitive but undeniably a...

"What's that?" Typical. Helen's awake.

"A Mark Three Travel Machine," I say flippantly, crumbling my creativity with a dismissive flick of the wrist.

Tuesday: Day Three

2.30pm They smell like old tramps' trousers but I've an unholy attraction to bric-a-brac shops, and Bideford's rich in them. One such mustfest saw Helen close to gagging as I rummaged tirelessly through the '10p to clear's. At the bottom, posing as a children's paperback, jacketed with the unlikely image of Hartnell in a flat sprint, my reward...

Doctor Who and the Crusaders. The Dragon imprint! Chas'll be green, I thought. True, not as green as my newly-acquired, 30 year-old, whiffy Whitaker, but envious nevertheless. Helen wouldn't touch it, but as I pointed out, by the 73rd page the curious stain was hardly detectable.

3pm The Collectors' Market was a more tragic affair. A pristine and much sought after Troughton annual – the second one, where the Cybermen appear to have interrupted the Doctor in dragging Jamie around the TARDIS floor. Like the Sirens to Odysseus it sang out its rarity to me. "£30" it called and I struggled away to avoid its cruel incantations. Helen helped me with an inconsequential conversation about a yum bloke on jewellery but I was quickly Delgadoed. Entranced by music.

"Jackie?"

The market's overhead sound system belts out REM's *The Sidewinder Sleeps Tonite*. I remember Nigel insisting they weren't singing it, but bouncing off metal rafters is Michael Stipe's repeatedly unanswered question: "Can't-we-wake-Tom-Baker-up?" I listen to the chorus again.

4pm *Doctor Who*'s controlling my mind. Catch sight of myself in another stall's mirror. I will be free of it.

Wednesday: Day Four

Congratulations for not thinking about 'it' since the Bideford Incident are put on hold when a boisterous Labrador went pounding into the sea after a ball thrown by a woman in a sailor top.

Thursday: Day Five

A beach shop browse brought a familiar sight behind the flip-flops. Looking uncomfortable between some faded Maeve Binchys. I give voice to its title and author.

Helen wondered what a 'porkornell' was and I flashed her one of his *New Adventures* by way of explanation.

Friday: Day Six

9pm (Shore Inn) Helen'd been drawn into conversation at the bar when I was approached by a man so irreversibly gruff and clumsy that he seemed to be suffering from terminal puberty. He wore leather trousers that were laced up both the front and back and sprouted matted Mandrell hair from his crown that was very reminiscent of McGann's first wig.

He said "You interested in cars?"

I said "No," but it made little difference as he proceeded in a tortuous description, underlining the various qualities and improvements from his second to third model. I was then told how his second, and indeed, first car looked before and after being unwrapped from around a lamp-post.

"Have you got a car?" he said.

I said "No," and stumped, he fell silent, sipping Murphy's and scratching his head longer than I thought hygienic.

"If you had a car," he started, "what type of car would it be?"

Right, I thought, the monosyllabic ice maiden hadn't worked. I'll try a different approach.

"A little yellow Roadster," I said. "A four-seater with a mock Edwardian body that fits directly onto an unmodified E93A Ford popular chassis," I said. "Fitted with an engine of the same model," I said. "With simulated artillery wheel trims, raised mudguards, a 105E Ford Popular radiator and foam cushioning." I finished my description of the only car I know anything about to the desired effect. He was suitably taken aback and I prayed he might leave me alone on the grounds that I was acting like a madwoman. Hence my dismay when he enlightened me that he had an old car magazine at home wherein it states where such car kits are available.

I recall Chas and Nigel, during a brief hiatus of their Bert and Ernie routine, actually agreeing upon something. That being, you should never mention you're a *Doctor Who* fan in a potential date situation until you've secured a time, a meeting place and, if possible, some of their personal belongings to ensure that they'll show. To reveal your fanhood any earlier, the boys conceded, is to have prospective totty begin to talk to you as if you're on day release. I attempt to turn this to my advantage.

"I'm a *Doctor Who* fan," I said.

Disaster. Turns out that he watched last year's movie and asks me to place several of his earliest memories. Typical. I've been aching for a *Doctor Who* conversation for days. Shame I was now having it with an Ogron.

Saturday

To lengthen a depressingly swift return, Helen stops for a meal. I've singularly failed to escape the Doctor, although I feel, like the Ogron, I didn't seek him out as much as he did me.

"Pass the salt, Jackie." I don't.

First published in *DWM* Issue 257, October 1997

"I've got a date on Friday!" brags Nigel. But how will the lucky lady deal with the stuffed Gell Guard?

Monday 15 September

It was the assumption. True, most of the male population gave up on me when I bought a Gromit-shaped backpack. An over-zealous bus door has since separated the head from the body and my resulting repair, which had more than a touch of the macabre about it, has duly scuppered any remaining interested parties. But the Boots cashier with the disproportionate breasts wasn't to know that. I'm a girl, more Sarah Jane than Miss Winters, so I couldn't possibly be buying it for myself.

"Boyfriend a *Doctor Who* fan, is he?" she'd chirped, limply waving the video I'd chosen over the laser scanner.

The fact that I'd been buying it for Nigel's birthday was besides the point.

5.20pm (HMV) Indulging in the pointless pastime of comparing other stores' prices with the purchase already made when my ears suffered a tuneless humming of *Teenage Wedding*. Nigel.

"I've got a date on Friday with a rather wonderful young lady."

All those syllables, I thought. He usually just refers to them as 'birds'. I was subjected to ten minutes of 'Nicky'. Lovely, gorgeous, "This is the one, Jacks", into Oasis, keeps a parrot, wears a nose stud, likes *The X Files*, slim as a stick, Nicky. Why was I having to listen to this so soon after my Boots misunderstanding? I had sought great comfort from the fact that Chas and Nigel seemed to be equally hopeless in finding that special someone that society demands.

I inquire as to the contents of Nigel's bulging carrier bags. The one not full of Tennants Extra. It became apparent that Nigel had done what he always does a week prior to his birthday. His bulk-buy shopping sprees, infuriating in their timing, serve to fill the gaps in his *Doctor Who* collection and to add a Russian Roulette type dimension to the task of present-buying. As the inevitable copy of *The Leisure Hive* appears, I shuffle around pockets for the receipt, pondering the femininity of the cut of my jeans.

Nigel was rushing. He had arranged to phone Nicky and departed saying that, if things went well, she would be joining us Saturday for the birthday meal.

A night full of Nicky. I'd rather draw lines on Frazer Hines.

8pm Making soft toys for the boys is usually reserved for Christmas. Nigel, however, has created a desperate situation. So he and his previous gifts – an amorphous blob known as Roger Gell Guardo, a Quark and a Zygon – should anticipate the patter of six raggy feet.

Mother, glazed after a *Corrie* fix, looks on as my creature, made from a Twiglet tin, a pair of her old green curtains and a ballcock, slowly takes shape. She's wearing that defeated look, reluctantly acceptant that her offspring has more interest in body horror than Body Shop. Was three years' needlework to be invested in creations such as this? Well, I think, any fool can make cushions. She knows the only thing I've knitted is a scarf. All seventeen foot of it sits in my wardrobe tightly wrapped around itself. She, and it, knows the child that so desperately wanted it was, by the time the skill and patience had been acquired, too old to claim it... But that didn't stop me.

Her son turned into what you'd expect from a male. And in many ways, so did her daughter. I'm her chimera: half-girl, half-mask.

She approaches my vaguely obscene construction and asks, with trepidation, what it is.

"Alpha Centauri," I say.

"Arthur who?"

Saturday 20 September

8.30pm (Chopsticks Restaurant) Again, it was the assumption. We were 30 minutes, two chow meins, a sweet 'n' sour and one House Special into a *Who*-free conversation when Nicky Parrot (yes, Nigel had become somewhat confused between her surname and the fact that she kept a cat) was expressing her disbelief that I didn't find David Duchovny "delicious". Gawping at me through panda eyeliner, she crusades to produce a fashionable male icon for me to find attractive. Chas could see I was clearly as bored by this as I was by the previous discussion of the Miss Selfridge Autumn range and engineered my escape by inquiring after the name of her cat.

"Cornelius," she said.

"After Roddy McDowall?" I begin, but her face was a void, not a flicker of recognition.

"Now there's an actor," enthused Chas, forking a prawn ball and gesturing with it. "Any mumbling suit can play an FBI agent but it takes real talent to play a tight-arsed chimp from the future."

9pm It was around about the banana fritters where it all broke loose. Chas and Nigel had started to catalogue the plot and visual similarities between *The Mysterious Planet* and the second *Planet of the Apes* film when Nicky, in one of those affected stage whispers that my gender deals in, asks me if Chas is also a *Doctor Who* fan. I confirm that he is.

"Weird, isn't it?" she says.

Oh dear...

The present-giving was going to give her little reassurance. Playing the Bill Baggs card with one of the producer's *Doctor Who* spin-off productions meant Chas had succeeded in buying one of the few items Nigel hadn't previously snapped up. I, however, lost points with Nicky when her proudly presented CD was superseded by a stuffed green phallus.

9.45pm "'Terry Nation's Turkey Creations.'" Nigel's recalled something he misread in a supermarket. He says it even had that scrawling signature, which had convinced him that the creator of the Daleks was called 'Nerry'. Fantasy kicked in as Chas suggested 'Barry Letts' Cheese Croquettes' and I 'Gerry Mill's Lamby Grills'. It was after 'Gerald Blake's Jammy Cakes' that I noticed Nicky's face. Poor Nicky Parrot, uncomprehending. She'd just realised that, little black dress or not, I was no different.

A fan, except female.

Monday 22 September

7pm Nigel phoned. He'd been arranging his creatures, invasion-like, down the stairs whilst the shelves were being dusted when Nicky popped round. I fear the assembled throng of stuffed terror which greeted her will only hasten the inevitable.

**First published in *DWM* Issue 258,
November 1997**

Jackie, Chas, Nigel and Nigel's mate are down the pub. But will the Chart Monster consume them all?

Friday (Pub night) 17 October

9pm "Chas," I begin, "you know *Shelf Life* in *DWM*?"

Interrupted by Nigel, who's brought a mate. James is exactly the sort of mate you'd expect him to bring. Swathed in hair and smoke, never without a baseball cap, he has eyes like runestones and a smile I've only ever seen worn by a Blue Meanie.

Chas is clearly terrified by him and a conversation laced with fear and alcohol lurches uncontrollably from subject to subject with unsubtle changes of gear which *That's Life* elevated to an artform. James compliments my earrings.

"They're little K9s."

He observes Nigel's left ear, perforated like a notebook. He's got three in tonight.

"Got anything else pierced?"

Nigel flushes. "No!"

"You got anything pierced, Chas?"

"I've got *Goldeneye*."

9.30pm James again:

"So, who's your favourite Doctor Who?" The ignorant but strangely appealing non-fan's use of programme title as character name results in a chorusing of "Tom" like the Beverley Sisters.

Now, as fans we all share the same inner demon. This monster, with an in-built race memory requirement to list and categorise endlessly, is an unholy cross between Rumpelstiltskin and Peter Snow during a bi-election crisis.

And unbeknown to James, he'd just unlocked it; it was out, unshackled and dancing among the Hooch. I had bought the *Book of Lists*, a tome recently published purely to satisfy the beast, but the creature, wanting more, seized upon Nigel's following confession, rendering me hostage to the situation.

"I once drew up a 'Top Ten TARDIS Landings' chart in the early Eighties" (Number 1, *The Androids of Tara*).

I could see Chas, like myself, trying to avoid the bait. He was concentrating his mind on nostalgic crisp brands again as, for the briefest of moments, I thought I caught his lips forming the words 'Outer Spacers' in victory. 30 seconds later, Chas:

"Mine's *The Tenth Planet*."

"Mine's *Castrovalva*." (Dammit, I've started.)

Table became a TopTenFest of landings, spaceships and, unbelievably, Tom's boots.

10pm I try again:

"I had a phone call from *Shelf Life* columnist Dave Owen..." to which Nigel asks:

"If the Doctors were Spice Girls, which ones would they be?"

James gazes at his mate in pain. As if he'd just slung on a pair of stilettos and popped off to the Ladies'. But this is a non-fan on fan territory. The Chart Monster, appetised, was hungry for some categorising.

Chas commented in fake disinterest that The Spice Girls were passé, then immediately nominated Davison as Baby Spice. I protested his right to be both Baby and Sporty. Consensus made Colin Scary.

"The trouble" began Chas "is Tom." Oh, how many script meetings must have started like that! Tom was also Scary; Sylvester, too, was found to have Scary leanings and with Troughton neither qualifying for Posh nor Ginger, it was clear that Scary was somewhat oversubscribed.

Chas says wasn't McGann's hair gingerish, but I said only in some lights. In most, it's blue.

Then Nigel says sometimes, when the lighting's strong (like always), Colin's hair reflects the orange panels in his coat. Although this is bull, all unable to think of better example. Colin transfers to Ginger.

There were, however, to be no arguments with Posh. Just as $E = MC^2$, Pertwee was Posh.

10.30pm Like Kroagnon, the Chart Monster belched a demanding "Hungryyyy!" pushing us to debate 'Great CSO Moments' in order of merit, and imitable *Who* mannerisms, a catalogue delivered in a style reminiscent of professional Bingo callers:

One hand on hip, one leg forward: Mary Tamm.
Finger rubbing chin: concerned Pertwee.
Hand rubbing neck: troubled Pertwee.
Lapel grabbing purposefully: Hartnell.
Lapel grabbing aesthetically: C Baker.
The self-delivered head smack: Tom.
Pretending to chew gum while smiling: Ainley Mouth.
Pointing at distant things: Chesterton Fingers.

"I'm reviewing some novels," was my final blunt attempt, but the revelation was lost. With the urge to list increasing, the conversation degenerated to a point which, if I'd not been there to witness it, I wouldn't have believed.

Pertwee's jackets.

Here's the thing. Although I've never consciously absorbed this information, it responds with frightening clarity when called upon. Evidently both Chas, and even Nigel, were also discovering this fearful aspect. If *Doctor Who* was languages I'd be bi-lingual.

Chas does a Jeff Banks touching movement around neck to indicate the high collar on the rust jacket from *Three Doctors*.

All echo "Oooh, lovelay." Like mums do.

I recall a double-breasted purple thing from *Planet of the Daleks*, somehow confirmed by Nigel, who hasn't been definite about anything for six months.

Chas has gone all pastel over *Dinosaurs*.

"It's powder. Powder blue." Suggested it was more turquoise but he wouldn't have a bar of it.

A brief discussion to determine if the moss green *Time Warrior* jacket was the same as the *Carnival of Monsters* one eventually led to what we were dreading. A mistake. Who would make it and when? It was Nigel. Colour co-ordinating.

"Didn't Pertwee wear green in *Green Death*?"

It was a race to get there first. I knew this one as I'd known them all and I was going to show off about it...why?

"No, it was..."

"...slate grey with red piping." Chas, flapping an imaginary lapel, had been even quicker.

Tried to rescue my position as Pertwee Jacket Knower '97 by pointing out the story's unusual presence of a Pertwee waistcoat. It was a short subsection and as a category, it didn't have the legs.

10.55pm Wonder if James'll ever come out with us again?

Must enter Chas for ITV game show *You Bet*... After the guy who can sniff out supermarket tea.

"Number Six. That's deep maroon with red piping," twinkles Darren Day, angelically blond, the nation's perfect son. He continues, "Name that jacket."

"That's *The Five Doctors*, Darren," announces Chas, to rapturous applause from Julie Goodyear, who'd presented him as her 'Freak' challenge.

11.10pm The landlord's saying "Drinkupperleese". Full to bursting, the Chart Monster's caught by his fur-lined hood, sedated and flung back in his box. He's a finely-tuned beast, after years of video labelling, voting for seasons, for stories, cliffhangers, villains, directors... To think he's reduced me to this – jackets and Spice Girls...

And to think I enjoyed it as much as I did.

First published in *DWM* Issue 259, December 1997

Chas and Jackie make a pilgrimage to a certain high street bookstore. But will Tom Himself make their day?

It was, for Chas, a near-biblical apparition that emitted forth from an unassuming door marked 'Private'. Had this divinity clasped not a carrier bag but two stone tablets and a staff, had he worn not a beige mac but a cascading robe and sandals, I too could've taken him for Moses. One hand raised in a welcoming gesture, he announced his own arrival, and the very floor did seem to shake.

"If God had a voice," whispered Chas, "he would sound like Tom."

Day of Reckoning

My queue companion and I (Nigel was late) share differing perspectives. I only realised how much I missed and loved *Doctor Who* after six years of successfully ignoring it. Chas, on the other hand, never went away. For me – with bunches, a hatred of classmate Darren Barry and a deep-seated belief that I may well be bionic – title sequence blue was but one of many colours. For Chas, it was the event of the week. A fleeting 25 minutes replayed in the mind, bedroom and playground, edited, exaggerated and bent out of shape. John Noakes was a kid, Chas said, a big, outsized kid, a daredevil, a fearless buffoon who, in the name of factual programming and *Blue Peter*, regularly attempted to kill himself before the evening news. Yet for all that idiocy and disregard, he never kicked evil's arse like Tom did. Tom was a hero.

"And what do you say to a hero?" By the time we were uncomfortably positioned alongside the Joanna Trollopes, Chas had visibly whitened and I, Tom's just released, unsigned autobiography *Who on Earth is Tom Baker?* in hand, was without an answer.

Photography section

Ahead, a voice like a trumpet resumes a *Planet of Evil* conversation consisting of little else than swapping jungle superlatives. This foliage appreciation, conducted with volume and fervour, was to smother a suggestion from one brave group member that it'd all been at the expense of the final episodes being played out against flat grey walls and a glass table.

"I suffered with Tom in that," spat Chas with something of resentment, and informed me, not for the first time, of a scarring incident that befell him in a West Bay caravan in 1975.

On the Saturday of the aforementioned story's premiere, a primary-aged Chas, excited by a late, impromptu holiday, became hyper, chattering and squealing like a gibbon until he was eventually threatened with the cruellest weapon in his parents' armoury: the denial of that night's episode. By five o'clock, with effort and a few angelic contrivances, he thought he'd pulled them back on side, but in approaching the caravan, had inadvertently stepped in dog's mess and trodden it from the door, up the centre of the van and through to the kitchen area at the rear. All was lost.

It's odd, I find, how many of Chas' reminiscences involve dog poo; he tells them as if the feet of all five year-old boys are magnetically drawn to the stuff.

Banished to the opposite end of the van, he elaborates how, not 15 feet away, the portable played Part One. The reason was that Chas' family often holidayed with another and their child, a girl of similar age with little adventure but cleaner shoes. She, on request, was to verbally repeat the adventure in its smallest of details. When the carpet was washed and smell forgotten, Chas, dissatisfied with a monster he thought poorly described, asked his mum. Within minutes, screaming in a tantrum of disbelief, he'd found himself once more banished to the opposite end of the van.

Invisible red string thing. What kind of dodgy description is that anyway... other than an entirely accurate one.

Then, laments Chas, being a kid and being a *Doctor Who* fan was to be hooked on adrenalin. When it's withdrawn, it was bad.

Leaving Non-Fiction

Tom, still unseen, becomes audible and my guts nag into life. I blame Chas, whose anticipation had transformed into a very tangible sense of fear. Tom laughs and every rich peal of it rings upon my large intestine.

We turn into Hobbies, where the great man can now be heard with crystal clarity.

"To Brian, did you say? I once knew a Brian who farted like a buffalo!" The queue erupts in hilarity whilst I pray hard and fast that Tom knows not a single Jackie.

"I fought for that man." I'd heard this one too, where Chas, using his Aston Villa bag like a slingshot, had fetched down Alan Higham for suggesting Captain Kirk was better. He returned home, school shirt ripped and, reeking of the dog's mess he'd rolled in, retired to his room to re-read half of *Giant Robot* in assurance that he was right.

With fewer than 30 people between ourselves and our Doctor, I realise Chas wasn't alone with such baggage. For my bedroom poster of Tom, I'm convinced, observes me. He's shared bad hair days, witnessed sad dance routines, caught me in what could be described as The Full Katy and, most tragic of all, stared in silent judgement at the mistake I made when a party accidentally renewed my acquaintance with Darren Barry. He still pulled my hair.

Media

Chas was, by now, virtually transparent when I, mouth dry as sandpaper, expressed astonishment to observe Nigel, not 18 places ahead, calling Tom "mate" and introducing him to girlfriend Nicky Parrot, who squawked at our hero like she'd just finished a cylinder of helium. Flipping closed his signed copy of *Who on Earth...*, Nigel caught sight of us and bellowed down the shop an inquiry as to where we'd been!

The queue reduced...

...and then reduced some more, past Trumpet Boy's entourage, to us. It was all I could do not to vomit over the table. Beaming through cheeks as full of smile as a pneumatic tyre is of air, Tom enquired our names. Chas, emitting an almost audible performance of the *Hallelujah Chorus* from his mind, nevertheless regurgitated his with Roboman emotion. I, no better, volunteered something sounding like 'Jammy'.

And then it was over. He knew nothing of Chas' battles, of my Glam Rock stomping to *Doctorin' the TARDIS*, only that we showed in a desire to give something back. To show that we cared. And that, although our vocabulary had failed us, seemed enough.

First published in *DWM* Issue 260, January 1998

Jackie's novel has reached its umpteenth draft. But the Prince of Romance wants a word about the text...

Saturday

4am (the dark places of the inside) *Although in an altered state from the few pictures I'd seen, I was sure it was he. Draped side-saddle upon a quilted chaise longue and dressed head-to-toe in a candy-pink ballgown, feather-trimmed no less, lay the Doyen of the New Adventures and Prince of Romance.*

"Pray," said the novelist in a voice that wavered over several octaves like a Dame of the Realm. "What manner of fan are you?"

I approached the figure in awe, only momentarily released from its gaze when from its lap was plucked a small but overweight, freshly groomed pug.

"A girlie one...who's written a story..."

The author's hair, whipped up vertical as if recently waved beneath a static balloon, quivered with excitement.

"An Orman! A rare breed indeed..."

I was then asked whether I wanted to fill the world with love or pain.

My answer – "Love, I suppose." – was interrupted, as was the novelist, by a knocking from a long wooden box that lay at his feet. A face caked in powder barely disguised his displeasure.

"And what is your message? Your lesson, your teaching?"

"It's just an adventure really," I added. "Like on the telly." That was a mistake. His presence, let alone shocked expression, made my words sound pathetic. Even the pug yelped its disapproval.

"Now you've upset Darvill." The dog was hurriedly scooped up within jewelled hands and thrust towards me as if he were a gift. "Give him a pat and tell him you didn't mean it."

The pug yelped again. I quickly withdrew my hand, asking if he had a licence for the thing.

Another mistake. The novelist visibly sagged to the growing disquiet from the wooden box, whilst the pug, snarling at it, revealed puffy gums, its teeth all extracted.

Then I heard the laugh, a maniacal, disembodied laugh that crashed into its surroundings, even stronger and louder, shaking furnishings as if under the tremors of earthquake. Both author and dog leapt from their seating.

"It's Auntie! Run, Darvill, run!"

I saw my last of them through clouds of plaster, the pug reaching an exit first.

"Jenkins?" The room fell silent to my name, barked like a command by a new presence who, although clearly a man, wore a knitted ladies' two-piece and hid a hairless bonce under a tightly-curled ginger wig.

"Auntie?" I asked. "Do you know me?"

"I know all my little ones. I fed you. Are you not a child of my glass teat?" As the figure approached, I noticed its left sleeve was empty and pinned, Nelson-like, across its padded chest. "Have you seen my commercial arm?"

"No," I said, but once more heard the knocking, and my eyes fell on the long, slim wooden box.

5.15pm "Have you been licking toads?" asked Chas.

No, it was only that the sanctuary of sleep had been invaded by the recent preoccupation of my waking hours.

So, it was on the discovery of the unusually matt *Eight Doctors* that I re-entered the twilight world of the phantom *Doctor Who* novelist.

In truth, my Hartnell historical, which started life as a Troughton thriller and is fast becoming a Colin comedy, was first conceived as a McCoy mystery in 1991, amidst high hopes of becoming the first female *New Adventures* novelist. Hopes dashed by a more literate Antipodean, I consigned my efforts to disk – traumatised, Ormanised.

By 1994, it had become a Pertwee parable, a devilishly original, must-read *Missing Adventure* that no-one else could've possibly even contemplated.

Nigel had thought of it. Chas had mentally plotted three chapters and devised a villain for it. And two months later, Someone Bulis had it published.

"An hour?" questioned Chas.

"A head-mushing hour!" I confirmed. For, like Sister Wendy nunning about over a painting, that was how long I'd postulated a single adverb, producing nothing more than the urge for a Wagon Wheel and a private restaging of a playground experiment.

Wonder if I can fit a whole one inside my mouth?

Yeff-fi-can.

A short-lived and hollow victory, as I fear that Wagon Wheels have dramatically shrunk since their Seventies zenith. Chas asks if I've ever thought the popularity of *Doctor Who* may be intrinsically linked to the size of the circular jam and mallow biscuit. Strangely, I hadn't, but it's just the type of mindless distraction that takes on a magnitude of importance when stuck between chapters.

So why do I continue when I myself have roughly half of each book series but enjoyed less than half again, finding the handling of their various agendas so out of step with the programme as to lead you to presume their architects may have wished to be writing or watching something else?

So why do I continue when the weightiest figure on display in any survey concerning the various novel strands is the one that points to peoples' disinterest? Yet most have contemplated writing and sending their particular homemade classic, with "Whashoresbowthen?" becoming a ritual phrase passed between any gathering of three or more fans. I have begun to skirt round such probing questions with a Deborah Watling vagueness, relying on "probably a Colin" to summarise the situation.

Chas says he's seen Nigel and Nicky Parrott buying plums, and asks whether I think the two-month relationship has entered a significant phase.

Sunday

7pm I've given Jean-Marc good thumbing but to little progress. My head, a matted network of names and plots, seems unable to produce one I've not heard somewhere before. Everything sounds like something, every thought requires confirmation, referencing. Every video, every audio scuppers an idea. Am now so confused that I'm not sure if the line I've just typed is mine or Sarah Jane's. Selecting published authors for hints on style and technique has only compounded the problem. I have become a *Missing Adventures*-osaurus'. The mere offer of a "waffer thin McIntee" and I could burst. Everything sounds like something Tom would say. Or has said. Are the ideas familiar because they suit the style, or because they've been done?

Monday

Chas informs me that, due to my enthusiasm, he has returned to his previously abandoned *Missing*, with considerable progress.

I might have to fight him.

First published in *DWM* Issue 261, February 1998

Mamma Mia! The party season's in full swing. Dare Jackie take a chance on a giant Womble?

Christmas Eve

8.30pm (pub) Arrive to discover Nigel's mate James contesting the merits of *Tiswas* with Chas, who's taken the floor on behalf of Noel Edmonds, championing *Swap Shop* "because often they'd interview *Doctor Who* celebrities, and Matt Irvine." True, I thought – but while being educated by a coolly-sophisticated phone-in with Mary Tamm, Chas was missing the commercial delights of a semi-naked Sylvester McCoy pouring cold baked beans down his underpants.

Christmas cards dealt, James resumes with:

"So, did *Doctor Who* do a Christmas story?" Specifically, he asks, has the Doctor ever met Jesus?

About to suggest that Matthew Jacobs clearly thought the Doctor was Jesus when Chas embarks on a flight of fancy which concluded with the most ridiculous theory I'd heard since the claim that the tin chosen for the Dalek box set has the ability to erase the videos kept within it.

He begins plausibly, implying that seeing as stories like *The Myth Makers* and *The Romans* got made, a stylised Nativity might have been feasible. Then, he proclaims, if *The Feast of Steven* existed, it would undoubtedly be watched on or around the 25 December just as *An Unearthly Child* receives its annual viewing around 23 November.

All's well until James mistakenly wonders what it was like. Both Chas and I tumble into an exhilarating, exaggerated re-telling of the lost classic; Chas illustrates the CID's hilarious interrogation of the Doctor, whereas I, tripping through scenes like Pertwee through syllables, detail the TARDIS crew's comic trail of destruction amidst the back-lots of

Twenties Hollywood. We finish, guilty, knowing any eavesdropper would presume we'd actually seen the thing, but expectant.

"Sounds crap," said James.

Chas, almost expiring in a choking fit, coughs himself back into conversation, demonstrating a loose grasp on what he purports to be factual science.

He expresses a theory, heard or read somewhere, that television transmissions, like radio waves, never die – they simply travel further and further into space. This being the case, the missing episodes aren't missing at all, merely out of reach. All that's needed is the appropriate funding and technology to zip yourself to some far corner of the galaxy, armed with a VCR, blank tapes and a decent aerial, and snatch them back. Of course, timing of such expeditions would be crucial to avoid the crushing disappointment of a succession of obsessive fanboys being blasted into the cosmos, only to return with a fuzzy *Coronation Street* and a couple of *Jason King*s.

I speculate television's head start may be explanation for the lack of alien response to any official invitation to communicate – their silence indicates gross offence at their continued misrepresentation in the 'new' Troughton episodes. Or conversely, inspired by the format, they regularly run *Attack of the Earthmen* serials on Saturday evenings – but fear getting in touch in case they get collared for copyright by BBC Worldwide.

9pm Nigel's arrival with Nicky Parrot signals the cue for presents and paranoia. Have I given the right homemade *Doctor Who* toy to the right boy? Chas' delight initially convinces until a sideways glance from Vervoid to Nigel's K1 Robot produces a pout that says 'more bits on yours'.

10pm Nicky's been talking at me, clawing at me; she's excessively tactile and my left arm's practically swollen with bruises. Shrilly, she screams praise at my footwear, then at Peter Andre. It was during a description of the fur ball her cat had just puked up that my appetite for her so diminished that I deeply yearned to be back in Chas' conversation, discussing the likely drop in picture quality as *Marco Polo* orbited Neptune.

New Year's Eve

7.30pm For 15 minutes we'd waited – myself and the Elephant Man (Chas, beneath pillowcase and coat, a costume none of us were sure if tasteful or not) – but Nigel's 'Disco Glamour Clinic' door remained firmly closed. Despite reminding him of the Fancy Dress Party's imminence, that James and Nicky'd be waiting, he had, he complained, hair to mousse, Aramis to apply, toenails to clip. We would see him there.

8.15pm (party) Unaware Nigel's been suggesting the Abba outfit to all. Nicky's an Agnetha, too – when it's clear at heart she's a Frida.

8.45pm The gentle 'diddley-dumming' had caused me to wonder momentarily whether my favourite theme had taken up permanent residence in my middle ear. Turning, I'm suddenly reacquainted with a giant Womble, recognisable, despite fur and yellow coned nose, as someone with whom I once shared lectures on the merits of the Bard.
"Jackie Jenkins. You used to draw Daleks on my college folders."
Finally facing my Waterloo, I acknowledge that I did. Removing his snout, Patrick Holland proceeded to recall further book-defacings and conversations that I, witness to how the intervening years and a change of haircut had

favoured him, would at this precise moment prefer left unsaid.

"In fact," he adds, "I can't hear the *Doctor Who* theme any more without thinking of you."

Dammit! This reoccurs with woeful regularity. Why can't people remember me for me? Has a diamond logo been placed at the top of my head which, although invisible to me, reveals itself in other peoples' photographs like the fatal slashes through David Warner's *Omen* snaps?

My burgeoning Adonis, persisting to reminisce, asks whether I'm still a fan. I waver, wondering if Jacobs was right about the Jesus thing, finding myself a miscast Swedish Euro-winning disciple on the verge of denial. Nevertheless, with gathered confidence, I concede that I am – adding, by way of validation, that "I still get my *Monthly*s."

There followed an awkward silence during which I never wished so hard that the magazine had kept its *Weekly* title. I blame this catastrophic *faux pas* on Chas, Nigel and everyone else who perpetually refers to *DWM* by a title abandoned over a decade ago. Furthermore, I shall hold them personally responsible if Patrick, wearing a face of acute embarrassment at my apparent over-familiarity, now Wombles away to some safer company.

"Do you do those conventions?"

"Yes," I gasp, back-peddling from the crisis, but in reassuring him that we don't all dress in scarves, I'm horrified to spy the arrival of Nigel who, framing himself in the doorway, moussed, clipped, scented, frilled and caped, raises his arms in glorious self-appraisal:

"I am the Doctor!"

My heart ceased its descent near ankle-level.

First published in *DWM* Issue 263, April 1998

Shock! Horror! While Jackie tracks Antipodean Mutts through a snowstorm, Nigel gets caught by the fuzz...

Saturday

Choose a job, choose a career, choose life. I chose not to choose life... I chose something else...

3pm Knowing the statistic that men supposedly think about sex once every six seconds, I wonder if *Who* fans are similarly blighted. For there could be little other explanation why seemingly unconnected thoughts and comments are rudely buffeted into insignificance by other more fantastical concerns. Consolation for my brain and the programme apparently conspiring against me is the fact I am not a fan*boy* – for if the first statistic is in any way correct, this, combined with the latter, would leave me with only four seconds of conscious thought, and with that, I may well find myself wandering aimlessly into the centre of the road. The trick would be to combine the two, and never leave home without Virgin's *Companions* book. Certainly, the scrawl on the back of the bus seat in front supports the first theory – and although it gives no indication why I should now be thinking of *The Mutants*, it does suggest several places where I could stick it.

I did, I confess, once own a copy of *The Mutants*, an Australian copy that spat and warbled its title sequences. I watched it at Nigel's with Chas, right through in one sitting, for what felt like a fortnight. I left that video evening sporting a crazed expression similar to *Trainspotting*'s Ewan McGregor leering through a windscreen. A year later, Nigel, courtesy of UK Gold, had acquired a less frenetic version which he'd suggested we view late one pub evening.

"What as?" asked Chas. "A terrifying alternative to sleep?"

I too declined his offer of a replacement copy – for, although stable, UK Gold videos aren't half the fun. The best you can hope for is a third-generation copy – and even then, a set's lines and contours stay as the designer intended. The smallest pyrotechnic explosion utterly fails to send the image tumbling from your screen. The sound, too, neither fizzes nor yawns in desperate attempts to regain control over scenes of extreme brightness. Nor in protracted moments of supposed silent menace can you marvel over the curious intrusion of white noise, a torturous crescendo reminiscent of an approaching vacuum cleaner. Only in the presence of colours red or electric blue can your VHS achieve that essential dodgy quality, and give you that reassuring twinge of naughtiness you seek by owning it.

Sacrificing a picture that blurs like a water-colour for relative clarity would be to also deny the global delights of the chattering TV announcer, most of whom appear to be directly wired to generators, babbling at such speed as to lead you to believe the station's entire output of power depends on it. To give credit, UK Gold has contributed handsomely to this tradition. Often at the merest echo of the closing titles, the announcer is gripped by a compulsion to relate information concerning the following *Blake's 7* story in such small detail as to render watching the episode redundant. However, compared to my *Mutants*, awash with Aussie ramblings, UK Gold appears positively reticent. That particular announcer, in a single breath, spans the end titles allotted him with deceptive ease, enlightening me and his native viewers as to several of his own resolutions to the previous cliffhanger – "What now for *Doctor Whooooo*?" etc – before dutifully imparting the time of the next episode and, like his later UK cousin, pointlessly revealing anything of any interest that lies within it. Then finally, and most teasingly, with Pertwee vortex well into the Technical Crew credits, he embarks, with brief directions, on an advertisement for the Australian Broadcasting Company's own shop, which apparently is jam-packed full of *Doctor Who* goodies. All this delivered with impressive precision to the last fading Chris Barry credit of the 50-second sequence. Who is this verbal genius? Find him, get him to a *Doctor Who* convention, put him in the cabaret; indeed, go further, make a game of it and once he's led by faultless example, invite other celebrities to try their hand.

Whatever, I know in some uncharted future when the BBC release their *Mutants* and it bottoms out next to a *Hercules Sing-a-long* that it will, like the catalogue that preceded it, not compete with the magical quality of a video that has all the hallmarks of being at the arse-end of a copying ring.

True, the Beeb's are official and focused. Kosher shiny boys in vortex jackets who don't need to be tracked halfway to Dunstable, play in monochrome only when they're supposed to and eradicate snow in all but your *Seeds of Doom*. But this once-enviable package now appears little more than a bridge between the fuzzing pirate copy and the pin-point clarity of the laserdisc, revived and waiting to expensively consign your archaic collection to history. Then we'll know what it feels like to be the guy who chose Betamax in 1980.

A couple of PanoptiCons ago I heard Nigel and two other fans hyping the new *Ark in Space* disc:

"Wow! You can even see the weave in Tom's trousers." Honestly! In the first copy I saw you could barely see the trousers, yet I know I've never recaptured the thrill of that viewing in any sharper, subsequent one.

"Nigel," I've argued, "if there's a show that needs laserdiscs and digital television like a hole in the head, it's ours. Inflicting it is an act of artistic cruelty, like forcing Ridley Scott to re-shoot *Alien* with the lights on."

3.15pm "What are you thinking about?"

I was reminded that I wasn't bussing alone. It was former Womble Patrick Holland, who had kissed me late New Year's Eve – and although I was later informed he was just being polite, I'd returned the gesture with such passion that only by late March was he returning to his senses. Panicked, I settled for:

"Whether it's Indian or African elephants that have the bigger ears...you?"

"Oh," he said, tearing his eyes from the graffitied bus seat, his sixth second obviously up, "nothing."

It's sad that deception had set in so early.

First published in *DWM* Issue 264, May 1998

Will Paris in the Spring bring Jackie and Patrick and Nigel and Nicky closer together – or must love wither and die under Scaroth's monoptoid gaze?

Saturday

7.30pm The suggestion that we watch something from the *Trial of a Time Lord* TARDIS tin was scotched by our inability to extract any videos from it. Nigel had taken to turning it upon its end and slapping it like a ketchup bottle before Chas, in front of a bemused Patrick, passed it to me on the pretext that I have "slim fingers."

"I have slim fingers," said Nicky Parrot, darkly moody, from the sofa. I passed the tin to her. Indeed, she is so slight, I thought, that with any luck she might just fall in. Typically, the uninitiated, as in the tale of the sword and the stone, retrieved the videos at the first attempt. Mistakenly, Patrick congratulated her.

"It's all those hours put in at the local gym," she returned, spiralling off in a conversation concerning the improvements made to her body – when, to any observer, it's clearly her mind that needs the work.

Unfortunately, the delay had drawn Patrick's attention to the mushroomed features of Colin Baker. I see hesitation. He waves a dismissive hand:

"I didn't like him." And, as if in a qualified position to venture such an opinion, Nicky joins in with:

"Neither did I." True, her argument held little resonance – she was pointing to a picture of Michael Jayston – but I was, nevertheless, consumed with a Jo Grant-like desire to dig myself out of her company with a spoon.

Somehow, I sensed this video evening was primed for destruction.

I sympathise that it must be perplexing to find yourself partnered with a *Who* fan, to know that you vie for your chosen's attention not with other individuals, work or recreational activities, but with the stringy escapades and tepid horror of TV make-believe; make-believe abandoned by them at a far earlier age for the harder, faster, stronger thrills of the thirsty pre-pubescent. What resentment, I wonder, is bred by the fiery interest in rewound adventures? What is the partner to make of the attentiveness, of the love, of the panic caused by a half-heard media report? What are they to make of a level of affection that they have only momentarily aroused in you? How diminished are they when competing emotionally with something as throwaway as a TV programme?

It's not as if Patrick's been force-fed. On the contrary, conversations are rarely tied to the TARDIS, yet the posters, the bookmark in my copy of *Fever Pitch* and the velvets in my wardrobe betray that I am irreversibly influenced and, sadly, already attached. On this video evening, he was to become (re)acquainted with the other man in my life – the aged, rather pompous non-conformist with the eight worst haircuts in the world – and I felt uneasy, knowing that both were to be tested.

8.25pm *City of Death* had been selected via a hectic and increasingly paranoid criteria that'd seen 26 years of product reduced to a package that would barely satisfy a BBC2 theme night. The overriding concern appeared to be the elimination of as many unintentional laughs as possible – and, shamelessly, three fans faced with a Judgement Day set about it. Within a devastating few moments, perceived classics were toppled, decades marginalised, eras condemned; our insecurities, fragile and stung by a hundred commentators, had made us cruel together but weak with those we wished to impress. Were we not big enough to square our shoulders against the possible sniggers directed at a waddling Magma Creature, or to brazen out one man's fight with his own bubble-wrapped arm? Was it necessary to reject *The Brain of Morbius* on such flimsy grounds as Maren appearing to occasionally sport a sponge cake on her head?

Fearful of derision, and suspecting that our loyalties might not be sufficiently suppressed to take it, we began.

10.05pm Approximately 100 minutes later *City of Death* was finished – and I knew I'd never enjoyed it less. By the second episode, Nicky had begun to yawn cavernously; by the third, she was almost completely under. I could see her head lurching violently forward like a spaniel on amphetamines – and Nigel's unsuccessful attempts to reposition her only gave the two of them the appearance of a bizarre ventriloquist act. In truth, it was for the best. Early on, after Patrick had exclaimed "Brilliant!" at the opening titles, Nicky had started muttering profanities about Fandom Goddess Lalla Ward. It was on her recommendation that "she could be quite pretty if she only did something with herself" that I thought I caught sight of Chas' fingernails extending, Cheetah Person-like, into his armchair. I was also led to presume, seeing as he sat motionless from this point onwards, that she'd also had a profound effect on his toes, curling them beyond the ability to walk.

Patrick, at least, remained conscious and largely unaware of the heavy surveillance under which I had him. Although with deceptively relaxed posture and head steadfastly craned in the general screen direction, I'd taken to obsessively monitoring his reactions, charting the contours of his face for smiles or smirks, with glances sideways numbering five or six times a minute. This, coupled with a forced grin – which I hoped might encourage others to find such insanely intense levels of enjoyment – had led me to resemble *Monty Python*'s Conrad Poos. I dropped this approach in favour of other, more conventional measures; small, unintrusive conversations which concealed cunning test questions by which his attention, or lack of it, could hopefully be gauged.

On leaving 16th century Florence, Nigel, without a hint of irony, despite his girlfriend stiff with sleep beside him, enthusiastically declares:

"We should do this again." No, I shudder to myself, we mustn't. Developed wisdom may have long nominated our chosen example as the story most likely to interest newcomers to the show, but it never revealed the vampiric drain their very presence has on both you and the original material. Of course, it's preposterous to feel personally responsible for each unfolding scene, but that doesn't explain why you do.

That night, Scaroth's head played more absurdly large in my dreams than usual.

First published in *DWM* Issue 265, June 1998

In which the Doctor fails to mend a broken heart — and a funny thing happens on the way to the Odeon.

Someone, I'm sure, inspired by the book *Everything I've Needed To Know About Life I Learnt From Star Trek*, has considered penning the *Doctor Who* equivalent, and although it will be a close run as to which weighty tome would prove the most useless, it'd be fair to presume that when dealing with relationships, the *Who* version would find itself somewhat abbreviated. Nevertheless, to take this fantasy publication as Bible, fast-track results may be obtained by cocoa sharing, becoming a Welsh Professor of mushrooms, or by spooking innocent soldiers with breathy, Perivale-grown riddles concerning the meteorological effects on your clothes. Caution, though, is advised upon the last entry; if overplayed, the erotic delivery can give the impression that you've verbally evaporated your own knickers. But while such a journal may burden my shelf with Tachyon scientific accuracies, enlighten me to which household appliances have polarities worth reversing and suggest several engineered scenarios in which to drop the blistering 'inverse ratio' put-down, when tragedy strikes, as it has struck Nigel, it would offer only scant reward.

Thursday

6.40pm Nicky Parrot was gone. This, the fourth in a series of self-analysing phone calls from Nigel, confirmed it. Despite the Doctor teaching him such words as 'genesis' and their meanings at primary age, despite the Doctor being responsible for his first waistcoat, first video, first doll, his follower had reached something of a plateau – although in the Doctor's case it was more of a precipice over which, along with Nigel's image, he was in danger of being flung.

"He has never" he protested, "helped me pull a bird...perhaps if I'd been into *The X Files*."

I muster my finest, calmest, social worker voice: "It's nothing to do with it."

"D'you remember Kim Wu?"

"Troughton haircut? Short? Smelled of bananas?"

"No. That's Debbie Dovesdale, who I tried to woo back with a remix of *Doctor in Distress*."

I recall the letter: 'Nigel's in distress...come back now, I won't take less.'

"Yes, that probably was a misjudgement," I conceded, but continued with confidence: "*Doctor Who* isn't a third ear. Many may not understand it and find its use as a shorthand for numerous other unconnected conversations confusing, but it isn't the reason why people like or dislike us." I was to underline the difference between being consumed by, and indulging in, the programme when the doorbell cut in.

"I'll ring you back."

I protested that I was rushed in view of catching *Jackie Brown* with Patrick at the Multiplex, but said yes.

I should have rung *him*.

Phone counselling whilst simultaneously buttoning a silk shirt had left me with a dishevelled appearance; aware, I opened the door ready to claim I was hurried. It was Nicky Parrot, pint-sized and grinning, holding aloft a straining carrier bag as if delivering a budget.

"Oh," she sniggers, scanning my attire, not one button finding its correct place. "Am I interrupting?"

"No," I replied, with perhaps too much affronted emphasis. "I was on the phone to..." I said 'Chas' to sidestep mutual embarrassment.

Nicky rustles the bag. "I've gathered Nigel's gear together; you know we've..."

"Yes."

"But it's a bit complicated...can I come in?" She passed me, gracing the kitchen before I could say another word. "You see, I know this is his." She retrieves a crushed copy of Past Doctor novel *The Witch Hunters*, broken-spined. "And this, and this." A Throbbing Gristle CD and *Goodnight Sweetheart* video. "These socks, I think." They had 'Carlsberg' printed around each cuff.

"Probably," I say.

"But these" – a paperback of Whitley Strieber's *Communion* and a Sheryl Crow tape – "could be someone else's." She throws me a bashful look, finally producing a signed Tom Baker photo acquired from last year's book tour. "He'd want this." 'To Nigel and Nicky,' it read, 'Happy Times and Places.'

7pm The phone's interruption was like coming up for air – until I remembered who it would be. This could prove awkward, I thought.

Nigel resumed, holding the Doctor under suspicion for removing, forever, the glamour pustule from his life. I, careful not to indicate the caller, turn to discover Nicky at my shoulder.

"Coffee?"

I shook and nodded my head in a manner that would have had people crossing the road to avoid me, but she'd retreated.

"Who's that?" questioned Nigel.

"Pardon?"

"Who was that?"

Brainwave. "Chas."

"Chas?"

"Yes...and Peter Cushing..."

"Peter Cushing?"

"...I mean, Chas has dropped round those widescreen Peter Cushings. High time I experienced his Dalek adventures as originally intended, eh?"

"Actually, could I speak to Chas...?" Brainwave now not so good.

Nicky, reappearing on the kitchen threshold clutching a mug, has the fortune to observe me, phone full stretch from body, howling Chas' name up the stairs. Barely containing her screaming delight, she erupted:

"Knew it! Chas is upstairs! You're just like me – you're having an affair!" I bury the receiver in my palm with speed and force. Although dumb with disbelief that she could possibly exhume any of herself in me, I sensed in that second, stronger than any other over the last eight months, that this creature truly had lost her return ticket. She was mad – and, as such, would probably do very well for herself. I returned to the handset and the escalating situation.

"He's in the toilet."

Nicky, craning her neck up the stairwell, squeals "Is he?", obviously impressed with my apparent lifestyle. She then spies Patrick approaching the door. With mock panic and suppressed glee, she offers to cover me, greeting Patrick with a weighted "Surprise! Don't go in the bathroom."

Offering her a bemused acknowledgement, he inquired who was ringing.

"I think" interrupted Nicky, "it's Someone Cushing." Patrick kissed me audibly on the forehead – but read disaster on my expression. For, on contact, Nigel's tiny voice had tentatively crackled from the receiver:

"Chas...?"

First published in *DWM* Issue 266, July 1998

What do Blackpool, cheesy flock wallpaper and a room full of decrepit grand-dames mean to Chas? Why, The Deadly Assassin, of course...

He was perched before the TV on a stool remembered as black, soft, PVC-covered, chrome-legged and with a crossbar that his toes couldn't reach; a stool which had, several years prior, belonged to the kitchen and would, several years later, vanish completely – but which was, at this point, his.

On it, Chas saw the Doctor die.

"Die," he stresses. "He simply collapsed in front of me with nothing more than the length of a Jaffa Cake box to distance us. I always watched TV that closely then. You could feel the static tickling the end of your nose. It was alive and, without a remote, there was still the need to have the channels at your fingertips." Or as good as. The three stations could be found by turning a large serrulated dial – like a radio's – which was optimistically emblazoned, silver on black, with undelivered promises: BBC3, ITV2 and something mysteriously labelled 'UHF'. The dial sat high to the right, above a yellowed, gauze-covered speaker. Sarah Jane cried in black and white to the left of it while Chas viewed alone, a glass of milk in one hand and a melted Penguin biscuit in the other. And although unsure of the meaning of such a difficult word as 'omnibus', he was, nonetheless, aware of the story's familiarity.

"I was," he says, "aware. Aware of my tiny, dodgy, worn, green cords and red paisley shirt, aware that the air smelled of mince pies and that Christmas was wonderful. At 4.30 on 27 December 1974 at an impossibly young age in front of an impossibly cumbersome television, I was aware of everything with a clarity so heightened and precise that it could've been yesterday – if it weren't for the fact I can't recall that nearly half as well."

Wednesday evening

The alarming truth is that through *Doctor Who*, Chas can gauge his life. It's a measure of near pinpoint accuracy, an almost failsafe system through which events that have occurred to him can be chronologically ordered by means of what was happening *Who*-wise. Nigel can do it too, and although others may consider this a rather facile hook on which to hang one's memories, it is, nevertheless, a method, and a largely unconscious one, which catalogues your schools, your holidays, your Christmases and birthdays, your Winters and Summers, your college and work. The programme continually offers reference points to your own existence. The result is that although Nigel recollects that being dragged unwillingly to the Upper Circle on 12 January 1980 concluded Season Seventeen not with an outsized bull in a skirt but with an equally grotesque puss in boots, his sister and parents, the purveyors of such torment, have all but forgotten it.

Recently, customising a small room vacated by a large deep freeze, Chas was repositioning a chest of drawers which bulged with personal memorabilia. I plucked his Denys Fisher Tom doll from where it'd lain, sandwiched between a Pocket Simon and an empty box that had once contained 'Doctor Who Candy Favourites'. Fisher's Tom was Mediterranean-looking and bore the features not of Mr Baker but rather, Hutch's Starsky. It was sockless, with incredibly small feet, and sported a three-tone synthetic stocking where its scarf should've been, but it was evident from the way Chas took it from me, fastidiously smartening its appearance, that the effigy had retained something of the original's greatness.

"Christmas present," he said. I muse that I'd probably been given my Sindy around the same time, but the difference between us was he could remember which Christmas: 1977.

Target books offer Chas similar triggers, each individual novelisation bound up with locations and personal history – the more unusual the purchase, the quicker the recall.

The Time Warrior. "John Menzies, Paddington Station. I stayed in a hotel in Piccadilly Circus, where the Coke sign, like a *film noir*, lit up the room every 15 seconds."

"When?"

"May 1980. We did Madame Tussaud's – six months too early, as it turned out."

The Highlanders: "Bought, ironically, in Scotland. We spent a week at The Star, where I read a harmless article concerning Michael Grade, the BBC's new controller. He had a vision, it said. August 1984."

The Daleks: "Town."

The Horns of Nimon: "Dover Hoverport, 1980. Family left for a four-day break in Paris, Friday 24 October. On the following cold Sunday I saw a wet, day-old English newspaper. Tom was waving goodbye from its front."

Pyramids of Mars: "The Lizard, Cornwall." '77 again.

The Giant Robot: "Junior School Book Club, where novels and picture books were haphazardly thrown on tables, hexagon-shaped and formica."

Whilst he was detailing *Death to the Daleks* (uncovered in a gift shop on the edge of Dartmoor), I was struck by what I've been largely denied. It's not that the past is irretrievable, more the state that it's in. Knotted, jumbled, contradictory. For example, I've no idea when the wedding of my infrequently-seen cousin was, except that I was older than six and younger than 12, or where Enid Blyton's *Naughty Amelia Jane*, my most precious and repeated of childhood reading, came from, let alone who bought it and when. That I stumbled late into fandom enabled me to check life against my relevant seasons, although admittedly there weren't many left and, like Chas and Nigel, the gift I found mostly involuntary. But through a deep pool of mental cross-referencing I've settled family debates as to when the conservatory blew down, of the 1988 Olympics, of a microwave that bust the day I heard *Tomb* was found. And if they can't recall which Auntie stayed a week too long which Christmas, I can, for she interrupted the last six minutes of *Greatest Show* as if it were her life's mission. Similarly, at Chas', an excursion to Blackpool's illuminations had been narrowed down to one of three possible years until he recalled watching *The Deadly Assassin* in a gaudy, flock-papered TV lounge with other peoples' grannies, thus fine-tuning the date to a few weeks.

A timeline of sadness, my brother calls it, he belonging to a world mass which can only, it appears, accurately account for its movements by means of public deaths and assassinations. Ironic.

First published in *DWM* Issue 267, July 1998

Jackie has stars in her eyes when a charity shop yields Doctor Who booty – but are these stars in even the same firmament as Tom B?

Friday

Having started the day consoling myself that I'm not the fan type who buys everything bearing the Doctor's face, I had, nearing its close, begun to wonder whether or not the faces which compel me to make a purchase were ever truly his in the first place.

I would like to view myself as a careful judge of merchandise, considering each item on its worth and relevance, leaving the belt buckles and Toby Jugs to others. The reality, I fear, is somewhat different – I've long ago abandoned this first, thoughtful, frugal phase. Jumping an evolutionary track, I've completely skipped the 'buy anything' second phase and am now hurtling headlong into the third and probably final phase: self-delusion and wish-fulfilment. This is a dark place where, working by associations, you find yourself buying cricket sweaters and paisley ties, long coats and spotted hankies; a place where you momentarily find yourself costing the number of paper plates it'd take to make the walls of your chosen room resemble one of the TARDIS' unseen chambers.

It is in this deceptive area where merchandisers are at their most canny. Simply by attaching the legend *Doctor Who* to their product they trick you, the willing consumer, to fill in a series of blanks which will make their wares glow with unshakable authenticity – unshakable if only because the largest contributor to the work has been yourself.

Doctor Who annual publishers World Distributors successfully operated in such a way for over 20 years – and, for a decade of that, made their annuals the most hunted of collectables despite the fact that only a handful of the hundreds of stories printed were in any way like their TV counterparts. Worse, the accompanying illustrations were nothing if not inventive – the Doctor was played by a variety of men of which only a few have ever appeared on television. Within 1985's annual there even appears to be a switch of sex, pairing Nicola Bryant's Peri with a Doctor whose face is even more girly than her's. Even in the pictorial heights of the mid-Seventies, the Doctor can, within the space of a page, run the gamut between Tom Baker, Robert Powell and, most impressively, Telly Savalas (who, beneath a curly wig, boldly adorns 1978's offering).

World Distributors do not occupy this realm alone. It is home to another, patrolled with a swaggering confidence that in itself challenges you to keep closeted your heretic-like thoughts. With its piercing blue eyes it traps you, slowly and methodically eradicating the true image held in your mind and sinisterly replacing it with its own. That I should find such an identity crisis standing stiffly on a Jilly Cooper inside an Oxfam window so recently after glibly dismissing Chas' own Denys Fisher figure was like being struck by divine retribution. For just one brief, horrifying moment, upon those sun-tanned European features, I thought I saw the face of Tom.

Normal vision quickly restored, I relieved the premises of the doll (without scarf, lamentably) to the tune of £1.50 and the chatter of the bantering staff – two portly pensioners, both soaked in Lily of the Valley and united in their opinion that Barbie's Ken was indeed the most handsome of suitors.

I was about to correct them when a second glance revealed the doll had once more regained the features of Hutch's Starsky, a metamorphosis strangely reassuring if only for the reason that that was how I'd previously perceived Chas' Fisher figure. During my journey home, however, even Starsky's features had slipped to disclose those of fictional Seventies TV lawyer Petrocelli (who's recently suffered a re-run in the wilderness of daytime TV), before reconfiguring again to form an early Engelbert Humperdinck. On my arrival home I was determined to unearth some reference concerning the figure, and located the merchandise section of the Howe, Stammers and Walker book *The Seventies*, finding a photo of the doll posed next to a Leela who, by the look of her hair, had just had the back of her head shot off.

With the toy's face now flatly refusing to even resemble its own photograph, I scan the accompanying text in the hope only to find a name halfway down to prove that I wasn't actually going mad.

The Seventies alleges that the Italian-based company, upon mislaying their original cast of Baker's head, opted, in an economy drive, to use whatever they already had available. Thus it transpires, 20 years later, that I had, on what appeared to be a fairly reassured day, gone out and bought myself a little Gareth Hunt.

Yet if the owner of Tom's face had just stepped forward, why didn't it much resemble the *New Avenger* either? Not to discount that it wouldn't, it's just that at that moment it was pushing more Bruno from *Fame*.

8pm Bringing both my new knowledge and my purchase to The Moon and Mushroom, I sat the doll cross-legged on a beermat. Nigel and James peered at the icon, the former convinced he caught a glimpse of Gambit. Chas was less so, and asked if any of us could ever recall seeing *New Avengers* figures.

"I had a Steve Austin," said Nigel, "with bionics in his forearm. And an Action Man with gripping hands and eagle eyes."

"Sounds like some kind of mutant," said Chas. I suggested that 'Gareth' came, perhaps, from a coffee promotion, and might – complete with roasted beans and dubious wrist action – have been obtained for six labels plus postage and packing. James asks whether or not I think Tom's head might still be knocking around middle Europe, causing me to imagine it re-used on effigies depicting the lead of a white, trouser-suited Mediterranean group that never cracked Britain. Nigel, speaking like a medium, returned to the doll:

"I'm getting Martin Shaw. I'm getting a Sixties Tom Jones. I'm getting Fred's face from *Scooby Doo*."

I was getting an amalgam of *That's Life* boys Chris Serle and Paul Heiney, but elected to keep the horror to myself.

"I'm getting..."

"Tony Christie?" suggested Chas.

"A thin Eddie Large," wondered James paradoxically.

"Getting..."

"Travolta?" I say. "Lionel Morton?...Lionel Blair?"

Nigel clicked his fingers in absolute certainty:

"Virginia Wade!"

Although further debate nominated Fisher's Finest not unlike Liz Taylor, Nigel's Wimbledon champion was, on inspection, not without foundation.

Match point.

First published in *DWM* Issue 268, August 1998

For one night only, Jackie's determined to be a thoroughly modern Ms – but will a Doctor Who spectre turn up at Patrick's parents' feast?

Saturday 23 May

9.45pm I had chosen a dress too short for an evening too long. Already I'd overheard a friend of Patrick's brother say that he fancied the tart and had consequently removed myself from the conservatory before realising he was referring to the food. Depositing myself beside a lemon-sweatered uncle with a Sterodent smile, I contemplated the impression that I'd planned to make during the evening...

"By the way..." Patrick had said earlier, "I've told them."
"Told them what?"
"About what you are," he said.
Being, as I am, without outlandish political views, particular religious convictions or lycanthropy, I wondered exactly what his parents imagined he was bringing to his brother's 21st. He clarifies his statement in a cautious whisper:
"That you're a *Doctor Who* fan."
That they should require such warning, and that I was told of it, seemed to suggest that Patrick saw my fanhood as something of a social stigma – and that if I, in an explosive fit of fan intensity, were to later gather his baffled relatives around a flushing toilet, dribbling "That's what they used for a Yeti's roar", then he had already apologised for me. Clearly, a reputation had preceded me. Any reservations remaining in greeting a roomful of people unknown to me had been dramatically marginalised, for I may as well now enter screeching my 'hello's from within a Dalek casing

before blasting their beautifully prepared finger buffet up their Laura Ashley walls.

Not usually wishing to distance myself from the programme, I had, for once, decided to play the occasion against type, so as not to conform to or fulfil any expectations. They would observe no fan geek in me. I would control my conversation, behave in the confident manner of an individual supported by four separate pension plans, be impossibly well-read for my age, know a person of great influence in whatever field the small talk might stray, I would be aware of property prices and of world events before they happen. I'd know of wine, of food, of a social elite, and have insights cobbled together from a full season of *The South Bank Show*. And I would, if any guest or relation were to be inclined to introduce *Doctor Who* into the discourse, behave in the manner of a convention attendee who, nearing the end of their interest, has only turned up out of a desire to show other people how stupid they are, and offer only light comment and a non-committal smile.

So it had been decided, and entirely independently, that I would substitute my planned wear for a power dress with a hemline bordering on the impolite. I would be Jackie from PR and Advertising – 'up to speed' rather than 'out to lunch'.

As is typical at family parties, the first room I entered resembled a wake, lined with so many slumped, pensionable relatives that any one of them could've been its eligible subject. Adjacent to them, a second group comprised obliged forty-somethings who, through cataloguing various exotic holiday destinations, competed with each other's wealth without ever relieving their gaze from the conservatory, which had a dangerously restless collection of offspring trapped within it. Making my introduction, I'd scored considerable success with Mrs Holland, who obviously thought I looked less like an inmate of *Cell Block H* than her imagined notion of a *Doctor Who* fan had suggested. Further conversations ensued, not one of them betraying that only three hours earlier I was studiously absorbing a book of cult science-fiction films, and that I thought *Yog – Monster from Space* was nowhere near as inane as it sounded, or that, moments before Patrick's arrival, I had, due to *DWM*'s chuffin' Story Awards, once more sought out the relevant issue with the hope that, in a further return to it, the results may strike me with some semblance of sense.

Unfortunately, no.

The notion that if one were to introduce a typewriter into a roomful of chimps, said primates would eventually churn out the complete works of Shakespeare, is one of the oft-quoted laws of inevitability. By the time I was interrupted, I'd begun to view the survey in a similar light, wondering how long it would take the same chimps to produce results as ludicrous as those printed, taking into account that the first several hundred attempts would have to be rejected due to the evidence of far too much thought and consideration being applied.

Whatever, avoiding an uncle's debate that my very presence had managed to U-turn from cricket to crop circles, I saw the approach of an elderly figure whose use of a stick gave her the slow, menacing march of a war machine of HG Wells' imagination. I moved to the centre, wishing she'd pass – but she, crab-like, mirrored the action. Confirmed by Patrick as 'Granny', she halted, resonating authority, with just a gap of a *vol-au-vent* between us.

"Just a minute," she shouted. Unaware of her volume, but not of the attention she was drawing, she adjusted her hearing aid before hollering "I understand you're the one who's a Doctor?"

With equally projected amplification, it was some minutes before Patrick could apprise her to the truth behind my mistakenly presumed medical training. As she retreated in obvious disappointment, I heard a conversation bubble into life from beneath the standard lamp. Two of the forty-somethings were trying to pin a name on the Second Doctor.

"Patrick Cargill," one said, the other only half-convinced.

It, and I, was out.

9.15pm "Bet you were thrilled," gabbles Mrs. Holland. "I said to David, didn't I?"

"You did," winked her husband.

"I said, I bet Patrick's Jackie's thrilled. We were only looking for the lottery numbers and there it was, on Teletext, all that to-do in Cannes."

Although admitting I was lost, a fan instinctively recognises when they're on the cusp of receiving vital information and how it feels to realise it has hitherto escaped them; shackled, defenceless, laid prostrate like Connery's Bond on Goldfinger's laser slab, with the expectation that it's going to hurt.

My gut, deep within, drained hollow and twisted.

"That they're making one of your *Doctor Who*s," she trilled, "and with a woman."

Afforded a room and television, Jackie from PR and Advertising furiously punched in page numbers on a handset.

First published in *DWM* Issue 269, September 1998

In which Jackie, Nigel and Chas give one of the uninitiated a glimpse of the tangled web that is fan criticism.

Friday, The Moon and Mushroom

8.30pm Nigel's mate James, not a fan, is often confused as to why we are.

"When was *Doctor Who* good?" he asked, rhetorically suggesting Pertwee.
"With Tom," we corrected.
"But not the middle seasons," disputed Nigel, revealing disloyalty. "They were rubbish."
It was at this juncture, with James responding to a judgement that indicated popular dissent, that Chas, always the more studious – and aware that James was not fluent in a tongue where decades are labelled with genres and credits – began his brief history of Time...

8.33pm "We have popular seasons, we have unpopular seasons, we've unpopular popular seasons, we've popular unpopular seasons, we've popular unpopular popular, there's massive, there's rubbish, there's madness. Nigel's dismissive 'middle rubbish' was massive, its beginnings championed by a young fandom as being hugely superior to the much-condemned squalid horror of the previous three, continuity-contemptuous, seasons."
"So they weren't popular?"
"No, they were massive."
"But not as massive as Nigel's 'massive middle rubbish' massive?"

"Ratings wise, the unpopular seasons were more popular than the three popular seasons."

"But the popular seasons remained popular?"

"Briefly popular, they were deeply unpopular. Demonised along with all who contributed to them, there was nothing quite so unpopular as the popular seasons. Yet this isn't to presume we have six unpopular seasons, as we don't. One of the many unconscious Laws of Fandom is that you can only have three unpopular seasons at any one time – with the exception of the Pertwee era, where four are allowed. Thus, the rubbish that preceded Nigel's 'massive middle rubbish' was no longer the rubbish it had once been deemed to be. Through this reversal, the popularly unpopular popular had been sandwiched by an unconnected season popularly considered excellent."

"Massive?"

"No, unpopular, but definitely not rubbish."

"As unpopular as the original unpopular seasons?"

"The excellent season was nowhere near as critically unpopular as the original unpopular seasons, but the unpopular seasons were now so hugely popular that the excellent season's excellence was diminished in the shadow of the unpopular seasons' commercial popularity – a popularity the excellent season failed to excel at.

"Now, remembering the 'three season' rule, the programme had only to reach its 20th year before the rubbish middle seasons were being considered quite excellent and the excellent season, complete with the two that followed, quite rubbish. Now, with the unpopular middle seasons challenging the popularity of the original unpopular seasons, the new seasons' modest popularity was considered to be not very popular at all. Condemned as idea-less rubbish relying too much on the past, the supporters of the new rubbish consoled themselves in the belief that whilst their rubbish may not be the top quality rubbish of the past – the past their rubbish was rubbishing –

it by no means looked as rubbishy as the rubbish of the future that was set to replace it. The top quality rubbish of the past, consisting of the now fantastically popular unpopular squalid horror and the popularly popular unpopular popular middle seasons, continued to exclude the original three eras from the competition due to their popularity being untouchable and their details unchallenged."

"So *those* had been successful?"

"Yes, but not popular. Research revealed the first two eras constantly battled to regain a popularity lost, a popularity only the unpopular years had managed to attain. The quality, like that of the excellent season, was considered excellent – even if, like the excellent season, the figures suggested otherwise. If the fantastically popular unpopulars' failing appeared to be the abandonment of all the quality, charm and variety that made the series' formative years so average in comparison, then the early years' failing was that they were far too clever and inventive to be consistently popular in the first place.

"To deal with the eras in thirds, it's believed the Second Doctor's first third bettered the First Doctor's third third – but the Second Doctor's first third didn't. Nor did the Second's first third better the First's first third, which was only ever bettered by his second. The Second's second third, which many say has never been bettered, failed to better both the Second's first and the First's third third which many say had never been worsened. Yet the Second's third third performed more poorly than the First's third third did, even with a high point which bettered the 'couldn't be bettered' Second's second. But the high point of the Second's third third failed to better that of the Second's first third which in turn failed to better the high point of the third third of the First. The better Second's second bettered 'can't be bettered' third is the third that causes the problems; although only half as popular as the second third of the First, the First's second third has the misfortune of largely existing – which the second third of the Second largely doesn't. Thus, whilst the First's second third had largely been written off and down-voted, the Second's bettered 'can't be bettered' has been written up and bloated – leaving, from our perspective, a challenge akin to appreciating the hole in a Polo mint, a challenge which, perversely, fandom has risen to, elevating the absent over the present as only the wilfully stupid can, buying into the hole rather than the mint and ignoring the unlikely convenience of an equation that equals 'missing' with 'classic'. Subsequently, to stress that this is where *Doctor Who* was good would only be substituting lips for buttocks and others are more practiced at this implausible drivel than I. Suffice to say that the Second's second third was the most unpopular third since the series began – and since the third third did nothing to reverse the trend, it is, with the exceptional exception of the First's second third, possible to view the series' 26-year run in popular decline just around the time it started. This leaves the early Seventies which, later considered unassailable through being unattainable, were amongst the first to be made commercially available. Attainable, they were considered later extremely assailable and so donated 'unassailable' to the truly unavailable.

"So, to answer your question 'When was *Doctor Who* good?', save a few weeks around Christmas '63, quite possibly, never."

"But it's nonsense."

"No, James," concluded Chas, "it's appreciation."

First published in *DWM* Issue 271, November 1998

AM, FM, am, pm...she's tuned in, turned on and wired for sound – but Jackie's picking up interference from an all-too-familiar source.

Thursday, 6.20pm

*"I may go out tomorrow
If I can borrow a coat to wear,
Oh, I'd step out in style
With my sexy smile and my dancing bear..."*

Singing a tale of either illegal animal exploitation or of an obscene euphemism that'd so far escaped the station's censors, the stereo, tuned to a funky 88-91 wavelength, belted the sound of Alan Price about the furnishings like a wet mop. Although apparently harmless, the drive time chat show can, with one innocent link between subject or song, cause a fan to fall apart with all the inevitability of *Terry Nation's Dalek Special*. Both are delicately bound; to undo them takes but the girliest of shakes – and such a shake was coming my way.

To hear the announcement of a guest whose career had, regardless of how fleetingly, engaged the Whoniverse, is to trigger responses to which the fan is but a helpless prisoner. Rationality marginalised, such a fan falls victim to a deep compulsion. Like Doctor Faustus to the Devil, I sold my soul to Sydney Newman; I struck the deal, believing myself to be in control – only to find, with the programme withdrawn, that the reverse was the case. A puppet to his teatime fancy, caught in a grip, a hold that makes one appear to be suffering from some obsessive behaviour disorder. You watch a decade's worth of *Telly Addicts* only to catch a few story clips that you already hold on video; what's more, you're so shocked when said clips finally make an appearance that you make a fool of yourself by struggling over the questions. Walking around the streets of your town, you start imagining you can hear the show's theme music emanating from other peoples' houses. When further afield, on holiday or visiting other cities, you'll pace bookshops to see if they stock the *Who* books you've already got at home. Sometimes, to vary the activity, you'll pick up a publication which, whilst not being a *Who* one, contains about its pages small references to the programme – references which, through being sought out a dozen times before, are easily located – and you'll find yourself strangely reassured to discover that no, it wasn't just the previous shop's copy which contained them. CDs of *Television's Greatest Themes* are checked and judged by Ron Grainer's finest's inclusion, those without falling prey to your disdain (despite the fact that you never intended to buy either)... I sometimes worry that if I were ever to face terminal danger, and my life were to flash before my eyes, that far too much of it will replay like a standard video evening round Chas' house – or whether, upon being treated to this final, free repeat, my last thought will be of the money I could've saved on BBC videos. Furthermore, in the confusion, will I view the tunnel of light associated with near-death experiences as just another title sequence? I'm so consumed by my passion that if I were to be cut in two, it would be little surprise to find the words *Doctor Who* running through my middle, like a stick of Blackpool rock.

So, as the radio guest seats himself behind the mike, the abandonment of my free thought has already occurred. Activities prior to the announcement of the guest's arrival have been postponed; only rudimentary functions – eating, for example – are allowed to continue, and even those are conducted in a trance-like state. You are *The Time Machine*'s subservient Eloi to the Morlocks' alarm; whatever will you've possessed, whatever strength of character you've prided yourself on – all of this has been over-ridden. You are trapped, and for what? For the given celebrity, promoting the Ayckbourn tour and the six-part North Shields crime drama, to completely fail to recount a single anecdote of how once, 20 years past, a fortnight was spent hanging from an Ealing ceiling or how, trussed up in a glittering jumpsuit, they'd once threatened pockets of better-dressed resistance. What's worse than the wasted time is the discovery, as consciousness returns, that you've captured this pointless discourse on some duff old C60 cassette tape you can't even remember picking up. To compound the sorry state even further, you know you'll end up keeping it due to it falling between a buoyant Bernard Cribbins and a McGann interview that, unfortunately, seeing as you missed the beginning and the tape ran out at the end, you're not entirely convinced is even with the right brother.

Yet despite such hindsight, as *Simon Smith and his Amazing Dancing Bear* faded to its dubbed applause, there came an introduction, colourful and eclectic, that had me repeating the ritual.

Had such conduct been uncovered in the mid-Seventies, I'd undoubtedly have qualified as subject for one of the era's dismally grey documentaries, the type with the film clarity of Golden Shred and the yellowed, dreary sitting-rooms that looked as if they'd been shot through a pot of it.

"Show me what you do," my smirking inquisitor, smoothing a sideburn, would request.

I'd narrate my movements, rising slowly from a chair, in a voice suddenly three octaves higher and as many times more pathetic than usual.

"I tune the radio in to get the right station. That's if it's scheduled. Sometimes you just hear them announced."

"And then?"

"Then I switch on."

"Who's today's guest?"

"Christopher Gable."

The screen, going momentarily blank, would return with the caption 'One hour later'.

"So," the presenter continues, "did you get your interview?"

I've resumed my place with the expression of someone who's been promised *A Clockwork Orange* but been given a chocolate one.

"Yes."

"And did Mr Gable mention his role in *Doctor Who*?"

"No."

"Why d'you think that was?"

A small paragraph of text appearing at the documentary's close would explain that, since the programme had been recorded, Miss Jenkins had contacted the production office, claiming to be cured of her particular disorder, but was unfortunately unavailable for further comment due to the unexpected appearance of Frazer Hines on that morning's edition of TV quiz *Crosswits*.

As for Gable, the prolific Northern Ballet's Artistic Director, Sharaz Jek appears to be a secret that he and I keep. Yet following his company's interpretations of *Dracula* and *The Hunchback of Notre Dame*, I sense interviews detailing his discovery of the dance potential in Robert Holmes' story, and how, after the heartbreaking Dance of the Magma Creature, he, Jek once more, brings the house down, twirling on a stockpile of Spectrox.

First published in *DWM* Issue 272, December 1998

The boy Chas gets tangled up in Doctor Who's greatest mysteries – but the truth is far worse than he could ever have imagined...

Then

For several of *Doctor Who*'s 35 years, Chas believed Jacqueline Hill was a man. Being too young to own the *Radio Times Tenth Anniversary Special*, Target's 1975 *Monster Book*, the only reference work he owned, was taken as Gospel by its frequent reader – its unflattering still of the original TARDIS crew suggesting not only that the First Doctor was squat and no more than a forehead, but also that his companions numbered a young girl and two men, one of which sported voluminous hair and had, through a lifestyle choice, taken to wearing a blouse and skirt. In other circumstances, the clothing might determine that a mistake of gender had been made if it weren't for the appearance, a few pages later, of a male companion to the Second Doctor who looked like he was up to it too. (Similarly, despite the insistence of Terrance Dicks' text to quantify Troughton's Doctor as 'clownish' and 'whimsical', the publication's pictorial reference offered images, photographic and drawn, of a man with all the Chaplinesque charm of Crippen.)

For several of *Doctor Who*'s 35 years, Chas believed the Daleks were remote-controlled and that *Death to the Daleks*, as its title implies, detailed their final defeat. And he told people, some of whom even wanted to know, reciting the facts as he saw them, plugging the gaps with inventions, papering the cracks with assumption, creating a functioning programme history from a few awkward, ill-fitting pieces.

For several of *Doctor Who*'s 35 years, he felt the pressure of his class at school electing him the show's historian; questions were answered with concocted surmises and a thinly-concealed fear of exposure. The expectancy of such office was intense; once, for a week, he fended off enquiries concerning the first Dalek film without ever contemplating admitting that he'd missed it. More generally, stumped for an explanation as to why the TARDIS disappeared instead of taking off skywards, he said that it *did*, and that it was the heat of its eight engines which caused it to fade from sight.

The TARDIS was the cause of much consternation; residing in Artus' *Dalek Omnibus* was Chas' only colour still of the craft, a solitary, Doctorless shot of its shell against a backdrop of snow which, it was concluded, hailed from an adventure with the Yeti, the one with 'snow' in its title – and, as the reverse of the *Monster Book* showed, this tale, one of only 16 novelised, bore the thunderous glare of the 'whimsical' Doctor. Chas derived a most curious conclusion from this sequence of assumptions – that the hue lent to the photograph wasn't a printing quirk but clear evidence of the 'fact' that, some very long time ago, the TARDIS' colour was not a blue, but a *green*. With the *Omnibus* bundled to school, the photograph, in truth from *The Seeds of Doom*, was paraded to the majority of 2J as proof.

Likewise, it was in recognising the varying lengths of Pertwee's hair that a Metropolitan Tyrannosaurus lost its claws to an IMC Robot, whilst a Dalek without shoulder slats could come from but just two stories, and a Cyberman, face strapped tight in a sock, from one.

For several of *Doctor Who*'s 35 years, Chas followed ITV's *The Feathered Serpent*, a children's serial, the credits for which named Patrick Troughton among its cast – but, since the thespian concerned was concealed throughout beneath elaborate costumes and oriental make-up, its episodes, Chas concluded, did not actually feature the actor at all. Similarly, he concluded that no-one would ever suspect that designs he'd sent to a *Blue Peter* 'Draw the Yeti' competition had been lifted straight from the covers of Target books; that smothering his treasured *Doctor Who* novelisations in sticky-back plastic was an act of preservation; that the best story in any year's *Doctor Who Annual* was, with a change of title, always made into a serial the following year (despite no past evidence to support this, he lobbied heavily in the playground for 1979's *Planet of Dust*); that the reason why there were so many photographs of Susan in existence was because at least half of them in fact depicted Dodo; and that David Whitaker's novel *Doctor Who in an Exciting Adventure With the Daleks* was the true account of the series' beginning (he was so disappointed to discover otherwise that later, when recounting the series' history to friends, he left the true facts out altogether).

For several of *Doctor Who*'s 35 years, Chas fought for his family to be united of a Saturday teatime, to keep the living-room congregation secure, yet it was he who abandoned them first. Shaped by an educational autumn of early *Doctor Who Monthly*s, the show had become a learned text and, as a student of it, he thought it best followed alone.

For several of *Doctor Who*'s 35 years, Chas bought rucksacks full of C90s and, in recording the programme, sacrificed enjoyment of it for worry that the spools would keep turning.

Now

When I entered fandom, late in 1986, it was so richly served by histories and guides that the basics of my understanding and knowledge of the series, which I continue to refer to mentally, could be consumed in the space of one fascinating day.

As for the details, I have no idea what a 'CVE' is. I know what it stands for and the stories in which it is mentioned, and probably I got the gist of it once. But at present it remains an unemotional, cold idea once had by Christopher H Bidmead; a term to be bandied about, filling holes where the drama should be. Yet should I ever have the inclination to know about a CVE in detail, its definition, accompanied by phrases such as 'fatal collapse' and a story code to be cross-referenced with three others, can be found in more books than I, and certainly Chas, would ever have thought needed to be printed.

First published in *DWM* Issue 273, January 1999

Munchies have been munched, hot beverages consumed by the gallon, plotlines filched; Jackie's novel is finally complete. But credit where credit's due...

Saturday

2.30pm One of the most beguiling fantasies *Doctor Who* ever sold me was the idea that I would one day write a novel of it.

Although BBC Books, like Virgin before them, are often described as 'sympathetic' to new authors, I fear my manuscript – now in its seventh year and victim to a hundred rewrites – is asking to find new depths in their self-proclaimed understanding. Indeed, in showing my final outline to Chas and asking him if he thought it concluded, he replied that it was certainly 'finished' in a tone that strongly suggested another use of the word.

The climax, a relatively new addition, sees the Doctor (Colin's) infiltrate the Tindell disguised as a Manx Harpooner. Despite the Mootie, late in the third chapter, and a brief incarceration with insane plumbers Hubbub and Smutch early in the fifth, this was a narrative highpoint. Surviving both Garris Boker the Glove Smuggler and all of Grubby Martha's starters, the Doctor had – due to an Officer's dismissal over an unfortunate misunderstanding concerning the hunt for a security screw – gained easy access to the Alpha Cabinet. There, through an unforeseen jitter on the node, he is caught by the Baltimores whilst adapting Forkit's Halo with a Static Bag and Diddler.

Being objective, I could determine that my novel lacked five things: coherency, old monsters, drug abuse, bad language and an *Introduction*. A weak passage in Chapter

Seven accommodated three of the omissions: instead of Aunt Web and the Twisted Pair, the monument to the Prudent now housed six smacked-up Terileptils with an earthy password. Its original occupants now debut later in proceedings, where Aunt Web and the Doctor attempt to unwrap her sticky nephews from around the TARDIS' Police Box exterior.

With these obligatory requirements met, the most glaring oversight remained the *Introduction* – the lengthy table of acknowledgements and thank you's which have come to characterise the series' many novels. Admittedly wildly premature and optimistic in its construction, I find, as with my published precursors, that although this presents the ideal forum to save on personal phone calls, it was also something of a literary trap which is, with each debt paid and hymn sung, in ever-increasing danger of becoming more interesting than the story it precedes.

Introduction

The story you are reading now wouldn't be the story you are reading but a better one if it weren't for friend and endless critic Chas W pointing out that, with very few alterations, the better one had, 28 years previously, been transmitted under the title *The Ambassadors of Death*.

Concerning the following, unrelated, treatment, it is he, with his knowledge of the potato snack, who inspired the Nik Nak Brothers and the chapter entitled *Quaver Point*. Special thanks to Nigel W for letting me describe his dancing. It is his movements which the Doctor performs at the Egg and Candle – and eventually lead to the establishment's closure. Also an acknowledgment to Nigel's many plot suggestions – all for the Third Doctor, and unworkable, with the majority of them being lifted directly from one particular episode of *Space 1999*.

Special thanks to Dana B who prepared and cooked for me the meal served up at the Carvacle Eaterie (the recipe printed in full at the end of the book is entirely her own creation). She must also be credited for calculating the number of pasta ribbons required by the Doctor to spell out the warning message for the Pendering Lord Tibbin regarding the Bantum invasion by Podger Seeds.

Karl H explained pigmentation to me, and all things genetic; his is the beautiful description of the three-legged Mousepork on the back of which the Doctor effects an early escape in Chapter Four. Alex G was invaluable, not only in designing the velvet pantsuits used by the Travelling Element Circus, but in choosing the Doctor's colour, inspiring the characters Geerson, Austin and Woolmicks, three of the five Timbrook Tailors, and for suggesting a subplot which – albeit cribbed wholesale from the box of a Waddington's jigsaw – helped considerably with both Peri and the 80,000 word-count.

Thanks to Jason M for all the unnecessary references to popular culture, and to Jason H for inserting them at the most inappropriate of moments. Of these, my favourite remains the demise of Garris Boker who, seconds before his brains are shot out by a Swissolent Blaster, laments poetically on his home planet, a cavernous rock situated between the Carrie-Un-Stars Hawtrey and Windsor. Further recognition is due to Phillip D for working out a continuity-sound explanation as to why the Police Box roof has, over the years, appeared both flat and stacked. This theory accommodates both the white-painted window frames and the St John's Ambulance badge, and should finally alleviate any charge of sloppiness on behalf of the BBC designers.

The convoluted Sontaran back-story overheard at the Carvacle is Andrew D's. Although these creatures make no contribution to the following narrative, it's pleasing to know that their inclusion will create merry hell for any future writers wishing to use them. I'm indebted, perhaps perversely, to Michael Grade, whose original *Doctor Who* postponement inspired The Cult of the High Aters, a collection of obsessive protest singers which the Doctor, disguised as a woman, joins in order to save himself from obliteration in the chapter titled *Doctor in This Dress*.

Explanation must also be given to much of the novel's terminology. All genuine, the pemphigus-suffering Cheiropteran Erectus is pronounced 'Kir-op-ter-an', not 'Sher-op-ter-an' nor 'Chair-op-ter-an'. Neither is it 'Crop-tin', 'Chip-pan' or 'Shirt-pin'. Similarly, Mussuck collects not the nightmare livestock derived from 'Moo-horrifics', but Mohorovicic ('Mo-hor-ov-i-chich') samples whilst the droning Boeotian is 'Beo-shn', not 'Boat-train', 'Boot-shine', 'Bowie-chin' or 'Billy-Ocean'.

Finally, apologies to those whose input I couldn't use, especially David C, who feels the loss of the Anti-Matter Moose – its conception, internment and eventual escape – as much as both the climax of Chapter Eight and I do; and also to a handful of *Doctor Who* authors whose advice I refused, oddly enough – despite their being the only people offering help who might have actually known what they were talking about. "A camel is a horse designed by committee." To all those who have indulged me – the guilty, the clever and the wise – my thanks.

**First published in *DWM* Issue 274,
February 1999**

Jackie discovers that jealousy is not only a green monster, it has one eye and indeterminate sexual characteristics – and curses Peladon when she learns that Nigel has enticed Patrick astray...

Tuesday

9.20pm In a relationship approaching its twelfth month, I'd mistakenly come to expect a certain fidelity, the solidity of which, it appeared, had singularly failed to anticipate that most obvious of challenges – the emergence of a rival.

"Jackie, you haven't got the *Third Doctor Handbook*."

"I haven't got the *Seventh* either...why?"

Unexpectedly, Patrick had taken to a study of my bookcase. "Shall we buy the *Third*?"

"We? And you see us ready for such commitment? What if we split up? Whose will it be?"

"I'm not planning on breaking up. Are you?"

"No, but it's a significant step." I told him of Gideon, an ex who, having divided the cost of a Pretenders album, moved up a maths group, drew four Venn diagrams with Becky Williamson and left me with the poster and sleeve notes. "Those scars never heal."

"I just thought it looked...no matter." The near *Television Companion* provided an ample spine on which male fingers drummed a nervous rhythm.

"'Looked'? You've seen one?"

"Er...in a shop. Yes, a shop."

"Which?"

"Armston's."

"The newsagent's? Armston's? The only *Doctor Who* books they have are two copies of Michael Holt's *Quiz Book of Space*, and they've had those since 1984."

"Somewhere else, then." A confession hung in the air.

"Clearly," I clipped, my tone as cold as Nyder. "Where?"

"It was at..."

"Excuse me? 'At'? Not 'in', but 'at'?"

"Now Jackie, I don't want you to get the wrong idea." Speaking like some cheesy TV trenchcoat detective, Patrick circled the room. "It was Sunday. You thought you were getting a cold, thought it best you stayed in, confined to the sofa, wrapped in blankets. I respect that. But I was at a loose end and the streets were quiet. I was bored, real bored. Eventually I found myself opposite The Moon and Mushroom. It looked warm, homely, inviting. With no more intention than of having a half and a packet of Cheezums, I popped in and..."

"And?"

"...saw Nigel. He was sitting in the far corner, alone. We talked, swapped stories, laughed, yes, even joked a little. It was Quiz Night and with a team of two we scraped into third place with a question concerning singer Rita Coolidge. When I first sat there I was only being friendly, I swear, but by the time we'd deduced how many years BC the Raquel Welch film was, we'd both, I admit, enjoyed more than a couple of pints. It was after the last of these that Nigel made his suggestion that we go back to his place."

"And you were tempted?"

"You know what it's like. It was getting late, we'd had a few drinks, his CD was playing, the music was low and so was the lighting. He offered me a coffee and things, well, just sort of happened. Before I knew it he'd slipped on a Jon."

"You watched *Who* with Nigel?"

"We only did it the once."

Like a cheap, chocolate Easter egg, I felt as if I'd been hollowed out.

"It doesn't matter how many times you did it, you did it. You haven't bothered with it for months – you're always too tired, you said, yet as soon as my back's turned, you're at it with someone else. Is it me?"

"No."

"Then why, last time we did it, did you fall asleep six minutes in?"

"It was black and white, there was too much talking."

"Well, tough. There can't be explosions all the time."

"It wasn't very long."

"Oh, please! I'm not interested in its length, or what it was. What was it?"

"*The Curse of Peladon*."

"Did he force you?" I asked. "You could've said no. You could've refused him."

"He was very persuasive. He was in the mood for something different and asked if I fancied it. He told me things, of the way it was done. He had pictures. I admit, I was curious. But Jackie, we can still watch it together, this evening, you and I. It'll be like it was – better, even, now that I know about the Galactic Federation, Hepesh and the mineral trisilicate."

"Spare me the details!... Have you thought how that would make me feel, to know that what you're doing with me you were doing with him only 48 hours earlier – the two of you, shoulder to shoulder, together in the half-light, humming the theme tune, sharing the in-jokes? I thought you liked your *Who* with me, and Tom-style."

"Yes, yes I do." Brazenly he scanned the novelisations – Pertwee's. "But having Nigel loan me the *Third Doctor Handbook*...I have to say, it questions one's loyalties."

"Look, who's who with the *Who* and with who?"

"Who's who with the what?"

"You've got to prefer one *Who* over the other. Now, whose *Who* is it? My Tom or his Jon? It's your call." Patrick asked me not to make him choose, hoping I'd settle for him liking one as much as the other. I said that was impossible, that it had never been done in the past and it would never be achieved in the future. Radical viewpoints like that could rip fandom apart. What made him so special? "Tell me just one thing. Was it more fun with him?"

"It was...different."

"In what way 'different'? Did you do it episode-by-episode with breaks in-between, or did you go the whole way without stopping?"

"It was quicker, more exciting. He fast-forwards through the notices on picture quality and even some of the closing credits, whereas you let it run. With Nigel, the beginning stuff wasn't important. We even chatted during the action and it didn't seem to matter."

"So you're saying you're bored with the way I do it?"

"Not bored, just a bit tired of going through the motions."

"Are you planning on seeing him again?"

"I don't know."

"But you'd like to," I said, then, matter-of-factly, "You could go wild, pick a Colin, a Doctor you've never asked for – *Vengeance on Varos* perhaps..."

"Ah...is that the one set in a labyrinth of traps and deadly games where torture is televised to the populace as means of entertainment?"

"Possibly..."

"You see, when I said we only did it the once," he paused, "I was referring to the evening."

First published in *DWM* Issue 275, March 1999

Can even Jackie bring herself to con an unsuspecting innocent into handing over a golden hoard of Doctor Who merchandise treasure? It is an interesting conjecture – but would you do it?

Friday

The Moon & Mushroom, 8pm People change little, and in recognising the older brother of a Junior School friend whom I've since lost touch with, a plan of such utter and underhanded villainy sprung to mind that I was both appalled and seduced by it.

Way back when, had I not been invited to the aforementioned friend's ninth birthday party, I may never have encountered her home or family, nor would I remember that one of her two brothers had been a *Doctor Who* fan. Also, if it weren't for the strange ability of mothers to know, through their own acquaintances, the changing fortunes, statuses, whereabouts and occupations of every classmate you'd ever spoken of in a detail that suggests somewhere they possess a flowchart on the subject on which your classmates' progress is marked in relation to your less impressive own, then I would have never been aware that the *Who* fan middle brother had worked, married and since settled in Germany.

Possessing this information, I planned to engage the innocent eldest in a conversation heavily weighted towards my devious intention – to secure for myself the finer treasures of his sibling's aged *Doctor Who* collection by means of a cunning 'devaluation' scam.

So, the elder brother and I are perched beside The Moon and Mushroom's bar. The plan was supposed to proceed as follows...

Fiddling with my pin badge, its clasp unattached, the motif would fall purposefully from my lapel, design face up, onto the bar.

"TARDIS," he'd point, accurately fleshing out the acronym before offering confirmation of his brother's teenage preferences. "From 13," he'd say, "he talked of nothing but *Doctor Who* for two years." With the conversation blossoming, I'd hear how the brother had bought many 'collectables' which now reside, bundled together, forgotten, in the corner of his old bedroom. I would wave my hand in a vague manner, hoping to give the impression of someone only momentarily interested, before enquiring as to the details of these 'collectables'. "Books, games and toys," he would reply, perhaps adding, "Kid's stuff" in the derogatory way one might expect from a disinterested older brother. It was just such a disinterest and ignorance that I was keen to exploit – all the while hoping that he wouldn't think to ask why I didn't possess the items about which I was going to display such casual indifference.

Determining the presence of jigsaw puzzles in this neglected hoard, I'd continue "Are they the ultra-rare, highly-sought, much-valued Whitman puzzles of the mid-Seventies which feature gaudy art showing Tom Baker being restrained or harassed by cloaked, pale-faced nobodies in a landscape of snakes and lizards?" Receiving the expected dismissal, I'd resume, "A shame, for they are priceless," adding an 'absolutely' to 'priceless' after a significant pause had required the sentiment to be repeated. "But" I'd encourage, "let us not presume your brother was mistaken in his purchase. Perhaps the puzzles to which you refer hail from that other Whitman strand of equal stature, *The Enemies of Doctor Who*, prized jigsaws from a range which trades at inflated prices owing to their rarity on the marketplace. Indeed," I'd say, ready with an impressive example, "I had a friend who, through good fortune, chanced upon a double of the range and, on its profits, bought himself a moped and two nights in a Dorset B&B." Confirming my expectations, he'd insist these puzzles feature only Daleks amongst landmarks of a shattered London, drawing my comment on his brother's misfortune to collect, not the 224-piece, card-backed classics of Whitman's, but the 29-piece, plywood-backed efforts of Woolworth's – particularly as these 1965 jigsaws remained so plentiful due to their pieces being much harder to swallow.

I would then segue deftly into a discussion of equal treachery concerning World Distributors' *Doctor Who* annuals, detailing how the market value and rarity of the Patrick Troughton editions have been grossly exaggerated, adding that recent research had revealed that thousands were given away as consolation prizes in Sugar Puffs' 'Win a Dalek' competition of the mid-Sixties. Furthermore, I would state that, although the original print-runs may be less than those granted the Hartnell volumes, they must be viewed in context. Offering a simile, I focus on the Singles Chart, outlining the decline in sales from an early Seventies peak to present. That a single's highest position was only 25 in the Top 40 of 1974 is in no way a poor reflection of the amount of individual units sold – and if such a figure were repeated today, the said record would be Number One, and for some considerable weeks. The same is true of annuals.

Perversely, I would continue, it's the Tom Baker annuals that are now the most highly sought. And, in explaining this switch, I call upon the rapid shifts of body endured by both Sarah and Leela within the stories and strips. Never once sporting the features of the actresses who played the TV characters, these women, often posed in a licentious manner, had long been believed to be the result of the artist working through a catalogue of ex-girlfriends. Thus it was unfortunate for World Distributors that, to avoid the charge of commercial endorsement, the BBC insisted they pulp the majority of their 1977 annual after the Sarah model was picked from hundreds to become that year's Ski Yoghurt Girl, and even more so, to repeat this action 18 months later when 1979's Leela was found to be a disgraced member of disco group The Dooleys, achieving short-lived national notoriety as 'the Girl with the Saucepan Handle'.

Armed with one further fabrication – concerning the *Radio Times Tenth Anniversary Special* and a warehouse that had, eight years following its release, dramatically reduced the publication's market value by discovering that the collective industrial disputes of 1973 had left undelivered to five expectant Northern towns as many cellophaned, mint condition pallet-loads – I decided to make my approach…

Fiddling with my pin badge, its clasp unattached, it fell, as intended, from my lapel, face up, onto the bar.

My victim informed me of my loss, but of nothing else.

"It's a TARDIS," I was forced to prompt. Two stilted sentences later it was clear that, many years ago, on a day of dizzying party guests and visitors, I had mistaken his family connection. Misleading a David had been the plan; talking to an Alex, a best friend of the former who had, through a change of schools, lost contact, had not.

First published in *DWM* Issue 276, April 1999

In which Jackie learns that one of the tiniest words in the English language can have an infinite number of meanings once fan paranoia has you in its grip...

Wednesday

The Moon & Mushroom, 9pm "No," I explained, jiggling my left earring. "They're little K9s, made out of Fimo by a friend who knew I was a *Doctor Who* fan."

He said nothing in acknowledgement but, "Oh." A short "Oh". A breathy "Oh". An "Oh" that travelled up with an exclamation mark rather than down. An "Oh" that was light, an "Oh" that was polite, an "Oh" of surprise. A gentle gasp of surprise, a brief gasp of an "Oh", a social, genial gasp, a breezy gasp, an easy gasp, a free and easy, breezy gasp. A cheery gasp that perhaps carried with it a laugh. Yes, in its expression and intonation, a laugh. A laugh of a gasp. The sound of the end of a laugh, the tired, exhausted end of a laugh that made something remembered momentarily amusing.

An affable "Oh", missing the "really?" that asked for explanations. An "Oh, really?" "Oh", an interested, absent "really?" that now was a question but still travelled up; an "Oh, really? Why did they take it off?" "Oh", a "What was the one with the maggots?", a "Who was after Tom Baker?" "Oh" and an "Aren't there episodes missing?" "Oh". Yes, it was a laughed "Let's discuss Doctors" or an "I saw a clip on a show" "Oh". Definitely an "I had a book, *The Invasion of Something*, or *The Something Invasion*"-type "Oh". The laugh recalled the fun of it, the being scared, the being young with it.

But it was only an "Oh". An "Oh" of surprise, perhaps mocking surprise. On reflection, the gasp was a huff, a mocking huff of an "Oh", a huff that said "Pardon?", a snort that said "Why?", a jeering, mocking, sneering huff that asked "Why?" A ridiculous "Why?" that perhaps, as before, carried with it a laugh, a snigger of a laugh, the titter, the chuckle, the start of a laugh, the beginnings of a bubble of mirth. A scoffable "Oh", an "Oh why?" of an "Oh", a "That's naff and cheap and over" "Oh". A "What's the appeal of a programme so slow, so old, a children's show?" "Oh". Yes, a scoffable, a "No wonder it finished" dig at the knockable, a "That Martin Clunes was in it and he says he's embarrassed" "Oh", a "Bet you dress up" of an "Oh".

But it was only an "Oh". An "Oh" of surprise – perhaps, I think, of honest surprise. But a spirited, honest emittance, an eager, robust emittance that was less of a huff and more of a cry. A snappy, eager "Oh", a bright-eyed and bushy-tailed "Oh", a ready-to-go, on-your-toes "Oh". An "Oh" of earnestness, of zeal and zest, an "Oh yes" of an "Oh", a passionate "Yes but" of a "Yes", an affectionate, respectful, sufficing "but" of a "Yes". A "but" of an "Oh". A "Yes but what about *Star Trek*?"-type "Oh". An "I love *Star Trek*" of a "but", an "obsessional in all of its forms" of an "Oh", "Don't you? You can't go 'til you do" of an "Oh". An "I respect what you say but this is superior" "but", an "I am superior"-type of a "but", a pious, sanctimonious "Make it so" "Oh".

Or was it a disillusioned "Oh"? An offish, "take a dim view" of an "Oh". A sigh of an "Oh". A disagreeable, contemptuous, sigh of disdain.

A haughty sigh, a lofty one, a piously keen, uppity, "hardly Tolkien" of a sigh, an "Oh please" of a sigh, a literary elitist's "Oh dear, no" of a sigh. An insolent sigh of a "no", a scholarly, "Science fiction's beneath me" "no", a vomiting, regrettable, "*Hobbit* unbeatable" "no". An "As a fantasy academic, you're a thousand times removed" of a "no", an

"Aren't you small? Aren't I clever?" sort of an "Oh", a "You must try harder, improve yourself, move yourself, up yourself" "Oh". An "I could redeem myself, cleanse myself, mend myself if I but took to his glorified smurfs" of an "Oh".

Or perhaps it was different again. An "Oh" of surprise, but of ill-fortuned surprise, a "bad luck", a "there, there" of surprise. A "shame" of an "Oh", a square peg in a round hole of a woe, an afflicted "Do I talk to you slow?" of an "Oh". An "I see you're gormless and dunceish" "Oh", a woe of an "Oh". A "How do you manage and who cooks your lunches?" "Oh", a "Do you have six fingers on the one hand and live with your mother?"-type woe. A wooden, mutton, dunderheaded, "Do you smell of toads?"-type of a woe.

But it was only an "Oh". An "I see" kind of an "Oh". A perhaps wary, prudent "I see" of an "Oh". An "I've gotcha, I know what you're saying" "I see". A knowing "That's fine, I'm open-minded, though I wouldn't have guessed until you said it" "I see". A "No, I couldn't have guessed" of an "Oh". A reflective, "Of the series I've heard as much" of an "Oh". A "Have you got tapes of *Cell Block H*?" of an "Oh", a "Does it attract straight people too?" of an "Oh".

Or was it a fan of an "Oh"? An "Oh" of "You're joking", a "You're joking, you're never, me too" of an "Oh". A "Let's start initially cultured, then get rat-arsed and slaughtered, and slag off the Beeb" of an "Oh". A "One of me" of an "Oh", a "Fan since when?" of one, a "May I present you with a needless list of favourites on the understanding that you can't disagree on one" of an "Oh". A "Have you, by chance, anything on tape you shouldn't have, or any invented news you couldn't have?" "Oh". A tactful one, a "Which book strand?" "Oh", a testing "Have you kept or taped over *Dimensions in Time*?" of an "Oh". Concerning the New Zealand episode find, a "Can't quite hide my regret it wasn't *Rider from Shang-tu*" of an "Oh".

But it was only an "Oh." Followed, seconds later, by another "Oh". A cursory "Oh." A yawn of an "Oh", an "I'm bored, when can I go?" of an "Oh". A "So what?" of an "Oh", a "So what? Not impressed," looking-over-my-shoulder sort of an "Oh", impressed-by-a-chest sort of an "Oh".

Oh.

First published in *DWM* Issue 277, May 1999

Rider from Shang-Tu? Mission to the Unknown? Tenth Planet 4? Fury 6? Maybe, just maybe. En route to the National Lottery show celebrating The Lion's return, Jackie, Chas and Nigel ponder those lucky chances missed...

Wednesday 10 February

11am *Doctor Who*-related news is usually heard first by a family member who, muddled by our questioning, paraphrases the report without, frustratingly, retaining any of its details. Consequently, being told they've found an old William Hartnell in New Zealand heralded a shocking revelation which would turn fandom upon its head much more than the mere discovery of a missing episode.

With levity, Ceefax clarified the situation and there followed, among those interested, much talking up of both *The Lion*'s recovery and *The Crusade* itself – an enthusiasm that hopefully concealed our failure to recall the last time the story even threatened to enter conversation.

Sat in a train, next to Nigel and opposite Chas, *The Crusade* had further intruded. Without the inclination to review its third instalment, or return to Whitaker's novelisation, Chas had, on hearing of the midweek Lottery show's intention to focus upon the find, secured three of its studio tickets.

However, it'd become apparent, with what must have seemed to observers ungrateful speed, that we viewed *The Lion*'s reappearance as of more symbolic importance than reason for street celebrations.

Uncovered at a collector's fair with a humiliatingly feeble price tag, and about as far away from home as you can get without leaving the planet, it verified our solid, if battered, belief that the status of an absent episode is more elusive than it is missing. It proved, even with regrets, tears and anxieties, that one day they shall come back, and we were not mistaken. It justified our prattle, the effort employed in vivid, verbal reconstructions, the hours wasted on wishful conversations. But most satisfying of all, reaching for Worldwide's recent video, *The Missing Years*, it made possible to fast-forward to an ardent fan's cheerless and crushing claim that it is unreasonable to think anything other than that there will always be 110 missing episodes, and shout "Wrong!...Wrong!...Still wrong!" as you play it over and over again.

Yet, within minutes of our first discussion, dissent could be heard. How telling it was when Chas, a month ago, pulled from his coat pocket an article cut from a broadsheet which had, at the bottom of a report that stretched the diameter of a round, Moon and Mushroom table, a boxed addendum listing sought-after episodes suggesting that if an alternative to *The Lion* had been found, *The Crusade* still wouldn't have featured among them.

Chas glanced across the aisle to the opposite window.

"Does that landscape look CSOed to you?"

Nigel asked whether I thought the Lottery would trail *The Lion* with a clip.

"Bound to." There followed a pause in which, in order to fill it, we all took a drink.

"Oh, sod it," he said, caving into the truth of the situation. "I wish it was *Tenth Planet* 4."

How different this was from 1992. Who, on *The Tomb of the Cybermen*'s discovery, would've wished for substitution? Despite worthier scripts, of which *The Crusade* was one, and clear evidence of more historically important absentees, *Tomb* was all-consuming. It *was* the 'missing episodes'; it had become synonymous with them.

Chas claims, as with the Snakedancers and the Mara, that *Tomb*'s reappearance was due to combined mental energy; wished for for so long and by so many, sheer force of will had recreated it – or, at the very least, pulled it 20 years or so back through time. Admittedly fantastic, after an exhaustive search of the world's television archives had apparently drawn a blank, it better explains the statistical unlikeliness of that story, above all, turning up complete and in such condition.

Subsequently, failure to perform the trick again has been blamed on fandom's inability to form a consensus over which story it now considers the most missing. But if fans can exert such mystic power, then the unholy mess created from our now divided preferences is expected to turn up ten years into the new millennium, with a rushed DVD release from Worldwide to follow three months later. It will play like *Noel's House Party* and be as much use to us as a chocolate teapot or a three-dimensional charity skit – but, like *The Lion*, will, I imagine, still interrupt the video schedules regardless of it being nine years since the final standard release.

I put it to my travelling companions that awaiting *The Lion* on video was a further example of *Doctor Who*'s past doubling for its present and future – and that with the technology already available, and the affordability that time would lend, the schedules of 2010 could continue to capitalise on the old without waiting for its discovery or accepting its current catalogue's near-exhaustion.

Having completed the range in the VHS format and, with greater speed, reissued selected titles for the dominant DVD market, BBC Worldwide – with, of course, much initial fan resistance – will inevitably turn to a programme of visual enhancement, extensive re-masterings which leap beyond the *Five Doctors Special Edition*'s timid exchange of effects. Proved commercially viable by the curious, less precious and a growing fresh audience, intelligently chosen releases could look in the next millennium as your Target books read in the last.

A re-mastered *Invasion of the Dinosaurs*, an economic exercise due to the prehistoric beasts' brief, now CGIed, appearances, would finally allow the adventure to be showcased as one of the most enjoyable of its era; a colourised *Aztecs* that, with a wealth of colour photographs for reference, would arguably be nearer to the original's intended splendour than the monochrome version its makers were forced to accept.

Overlay a new Skarasen, Myrka and Kroll; drop in the shadows, the claustrophobia missing from *Tomb*. Throw colour and reflection at flatly-lit studios. Give Metebelis 3 its blue, Karn its thunder and Sarn its burn; like the fledgling techniques employed on *Survival*'s Cheetah Planet, fill its skies with fire and our vision with the haze of its heat. Cloud the heavens of Logopolis with the rush of entropy, cast darkness in its pathways, lend it weight, tremble and agitate and corrode its image. Re-edit and re-score – productions like *Battlefield* and *Silver Nemesis* need fewer scenes, not more. Top and tail them, blend them, overcut and underrun them. Like Lovett Bickford, *The Leisure Hive*'s director, abandon the stretchmarks of 25 minutes if better is achievable in less.

"If I won four million..." began Chas. But his expectations were interrupted by Nigel's wanting Carol Smillie.

Oh, so many crusades.

First published in *DWM* Issue 278, June 1999

It's the party of the season. A Zarbi has tempted Chas to turn gigolo, and there's six feet of unmitigated evil in the coats room...

Claire was a classmate from junior school. Time had dwindled our friendship to an acquaintance but we never forgot each other when it came to Christmas cards and birthday celebrations. Having attended her previous parties single, I, at her invitation to "bring someone", informed her it would be boyfriend Patrick. Patrick, though, had recently been increasingly elusive, unavailability currently his strongest characteristic. Via the phone, he stressed he was otherwise committed but that, at some time, "we really should talk."

I faced his suggestion to take workmate Helen with reluctance. Previously, arriving alone had drawn from the gathering an almost tangible air of confirmation.

I thought of Chas. Rang him, asking if he'd pretend to be Patrick. "As we've been going out for over a year it wouldn't appear odd if we weren't tactile. For a friend," I pleaded. "For a Harlequin die-cast miniature." But he wouldn't be persuaded.

Nigel was easier, though not without risk. I've yet to attend a party where drink hasn't persuaded him to burst forth with an unsolicited, tuneless but word-perfect rendition of the theme to the *Pink Panther* cartoon.

Saturday 24 April

11.17pm Nigel had rung. He would be delayed. I arrived informing more people than necessary that Patrick was joining me later. Following a lapse of 45 minutes, he did. It was Chas.

"This is for a Zarbi. Three pounds, Harlequin code DW102."

"You can't be Patrick!"

"The arms are a bit long, but I can always take them in a bit."

"But I've asked Nigel to be Patrick! I can't have two Patricks!" Leading him away, I began an explanation that Claire, calling us back, interrupted.

"Who's he?" Nigel had arrived, protesting his Patrickness. "Is he a gatecrasher?"

"Not exactly," corrected Chas. "He's not so much one of them...as one of me."

If I was to be taken from this world, now would seem appropriate.

"Oh no, no, no!" argued Nigel. "I'm sorry, my dear. I hate to be contrary but I can see he's a bit confused, and I do feel you should have the correct explanation. You see, Claire, – I may call you Claire, mayn't I? – he's one of me."

"You're both Patricks?"

"Well, quite. Well, not quite. Not just Patricks...we're the same Patrick!"

"Oh, please!" I interrupted. "You're only confusing my friend."

"I am he, and he is me," pointed Chas.

"And we are all together," I concluded.

Claire studied me. "Well...aren't you the dark horse?"

Smiling thinly, I excused myself. "Claire, Patricks, I've a room yet to circulate." Walking backwards into it, I requested not to be found.

Escape to Danger

11.39pm Packed to capacity, the corner of my seclusion was taken.

"So, Jackie, we meet again." Darren Barry, my junior school nemesis. We hated each other with passion. Even aged nine, the only reason either of us attended school was to make the other's life miserable. He'd pull my hair, I'd nick his daps. He'd stuff my bag with grass and leaves, I'd frisbee his sandwiches high upon the art block roof. He'd laugh at my karate-chopping, playing *Charlie's Angels*, despite the obvious talent required to play that show individually. I'd laugh at his bow-legged *Planet of the Apes* enactments, shouting as he entered class "Are you still doing it, Darren, as I can't tell the difference." "You're not really like a girl," he'd say. "You are," I'd answer. "You're the biggest girl in the school."

How stupid. How idiotic to forget it was a party of Claire's that'd previously reintroduced me, after an interval of eleven years, to my rival in torment. Darren. Short dark hair, black canvas walking boots, black denim, black shirt, black heart. Six foot of evil to my five eight. We had talked, smirked and finally laughed. While lessons and teachers were half-forgotten, each individual hell we caused the other survived with sharpest clarity. It was our common bond, we were bound together in darkness. We'd made up, perhaps too much.

And here he was again, following a further gap of three years, addressing me like a character from my own video collection.

"You appear surprised to see me."

"More disappointed. I rather hoped I'd seen the last of you."

"At a party of Claire's? You have been naive. You look thirsty..."

"I am."

"...and sexy."

"I still hate you, Darren."

"Of course. And I you. It's what we do."

"Good," I said. "As long as we understand each other. There's enough uncertainty in the universe as it is."

He laughed, asking if I still had a poster of Tom Baker above the bed, and whether I remembered him questioning if it was some form of protection. He leaned forward.

"Are you here with anyone?"

"Don't play with my hair."

"Sorry. Well?"

"I snapped all the pencils in your Kevin Keegan pencil case," I evaded. "I used to draw a face in the thick school custard and cut at it, pretending it was yours." Illustrating, I criss-crossed his face with my finger; he kissed it as the nail brushed his lips.

"I spent weekends cutting you down with a light sabre, yet Monday morning you came back."

"A hundred times stronger," I answered.

"I loathed you. I'm still obsessed with loathing you. I watched that American *Doctor Who* because I knew you would be, and I hoped you hated it." He kissed my forehead.

"I hoped it'd run forever and that you, and all those who'd ever taken a jibe at me and it, would picture me delighted. Happy and partying hard. I still torment you, yes?" I kissed him back. "If out, you see *Doctor Who* printed on a book, I haunt you, yes? If answering a trivia quiz question or catching Peter Davison in a hopeless comedy, I fill your mind."

"Yes." He grabbed my waist. "I slaughter it in conversation through knowing you. I hate it because I love to hate you. You're the most 'like me' person I've ever known. You pressed drawing pins into my bike tyres. And three years ago, leaving as you slept, my bootlaces broke. They'd been snipped at with scissors."

"And I found my *Evil of the Daleks* cassettes in the toaster. Which room has Claire put the coats?" I asked. "Let's hate each other in there."

00:22am Claire was talking through the jar of the door.
"There's another Patrick here."
"Two minutes," I said.
I trotted down the stairs, tidying myself, greeting the real Patrick in the hallway. "What are you doing here?"
"Celebrating, hopefully. I've just heard. It's why I've been so busy. Training courses, etcetera. It's promotion and transfer, hotel manager."
"Transfer?"
"To Leeds. And I want you to come with me."
"Four minutes," I said, pelting back upstairs, crashing into Chas on the landing.
"Don't go, Jackie. To Leeds, I mean."
I continued to the coat room, closing the door behind me. In the dark silence, I hated Darren one final time.
"I'll get in touch," I promised, and rejoined the landing. Darren was there.
"I've just left that room."
"What?"
Twisting the handle, he let the door swing naturally open. There was singing:
"Yes, he's the Pink Panther, the rinky-dink Panther, and it's as plain as your nose..."

First published in _DWM_ Issue 279, June 1999

Three weeks had passed since Jackie tumbled with her childhood nemesis. Disaster is imminent – but first, a few home truths will out...

Three weeks after Claire's party

It was occasionally the wont of my workmate Helen to extend our office hours by frequenting the bar she considered her luckiest. It was a description not without justification – although lately, she'd found it to perform poorly. Nevertheless, while I'd been ordering drinks, the seating arrangements had changed. Helen was in mine and a male had been persuaded to sit in hers. So, grabbing a spare, I decided to make my presence brief. But during a conversation concerning little, it became apparent that, when Helen had introduced me, confusion had arisen; Helen had ended up being addressed by my name, and I by hers. Helen, amused, continued to attribute her name to me whenever the discourse allowed. She was flirting, of course – the deception was part of it. Unfortunately for me, her companion's focus plainly rested rather less upon her than she hoped. She took action.

"That top's very flattering, Helen," she said. "It makes you appear less broad in the shoulders."

I glanced at her guest. "Would you believe we're in public relations?" I asked, adding, bluntly: "Like advertising, it often causes us to trick people. Jackie's quite a professional."

Helen glared at me. "And wearing your hair away from your face is more youthful for you."

I decided that, having been given her name, I'd also take her part. "Thank you, Jackie. It's an attempt to revive my appeal that, as I've begun to appear more dated, I've found to have wavered slightly." I'd taken her part. Helen bit back, taking mine, patting the arm of the male for attention.

"Have I mentioned that at a recent party I compromised a relationship with an acquaintance from my past – and further, I'd acquired his mobile phone?" She retrieved it from my coat pocket, placing it down on the table as both illustration and proof.

"Have I made the point," I responded, "that when recounting stories I'm inclined to sensationalise, a practice gaining me an unfortunate reputation not entirely appreciated by my work colleagues?"

"The idea that my exit from the party was rushed is acceptable," Helen continued, "but my claim that the darkened conditions had caused me to clumsily uptip my bag, and that mistakenly I'd gathered up Darren's mobile phone, rather than my own, in consequence has, amongst those I've told, been greeted with scepticism. The notion that I've not been inclined to return it has been met with equal suspicion."

"Have I mentioned, being only interested in the salacious, that I entirely fail to understand your theory that Darren and yourself are a 'once every four years' thing?" I said. "That contact would deprive you both of the feelings of hurt, hate and betrayal that require such time to fester? That a history exists between you that makes six year-olds of adults? That you're back in the playground, filling his shoes with mud, back in assembly, clutching handfuls of chalk dust, back wearing a *Bionic Woman* T-shirt, back trembling, fixed in the stare of Mrs Stone, being blamed for the tomato slices flicked and slowly sliding down the dining hall window – when it was he, Darren, grinning behind you, who was guilty? I fail to understand that he is your sworn enemy and returning mobile phones is not the sort of activity in which sworn enemies partake – well, not without first hollowing it out and filling it with peas."

Helen changed tack. "Have I mentioned I'm a *Doctor Who* fan? At work, when I think no-one's looking, I pretend all the keyboards and computer screens are the controls to a spaceship. I've been caught punching the 'return' key and shouting, 'If I can just get the TARDIS free of the Time Corridor!' I enhance the functions of mechanical appliances by humming my own sci-fi noises. I can't pick up a stapler without thinking it's a laser gun, or operate calculators and hand remotes without imagining I've programmed a robot, or opened a secret panel in a solid wall of brick."

"Well," I interrupted, "I haven't really the depth of character or imaginary scope for such an interest. I'm far too busy working my way through the male population to apply my mind to anything above the waist."

"Whereas I'm reading," Helen returned, "but only *Doctor Who* books. I'm terribly insular and obsessively ordered. I cannot understand how people can exist knowing they have magazines where the one on top is of an earlier edition than the one underneath."

"I'd buy *Hello* if I didn't find the pictures so taxing..."

"And television," Helen persisted. "*Doctor Who*, of course, preferably old black and white. The slower the better, as I believe my stamina for such programmes is perceived as a sign of intelligence and an appreciator of a more literate culture. Also, in watching programmes made before my birth by choice, I hope to imply that I'm an oracle of the medium and, as such, have licence to patronise others on the workings of television. Where, in truth, my over-exposure to just one programme renders my knowledge archaic, commonplace and of no use to man nor beast."

"If it's not glossy, big budget, made in the last five years, forget it," I sighed, "particularly if it makes you think and features characterful actors who I don't fancy. It's pointless stating TV's the most powerful artform when I'm only interested in who's drinking at the Rovers."

"Did you know," spat Helen, "that John Cleese was once in *Doctor Who*? You won't wish for it, but I can tell you the names of everyone who was in *Doctor Who*, including a few you might have actually heard of." She swung round and then back again in mock interruption. "Oh, I'm sorry, I know I was talking to you but I thought I heard someone express a preference for Pertwee. They're completely wrong. Everyone knows Tom Baker was the best. It makes me so unreasonably agitated when people disagree with me about *Doctor Who*. They're not fans, they don't have the right!" She waved her hand dismissively. "You're lucky I'm even talking to you. If my *Doctor Who* friends were here, I'd be talking to them instead, making allusions to things you'd never understand whilst choosing not to explain them until, eventually, you'd be so out of the conversation that you might as well not be there."

"Of course," I quipped, "if I'd anything decent to offer originally, I'd never have been left out of the conversation in the first place. I'd be able to introduce subjects in a witty, interesting manner that would arrest the attention of those present and manoeuvre the discussion into other areas."

"And finally," she blazed, "at the end of the evening, I'd apologise for talking too much about *Doctor Who* before expressing token disquietude over alienating and probably boring you – despite proceeding to do exactly the same the next time."

"I bore men anyway," I blistered.

"I dress up as them," she flung back.

The trill of the mobile phone interrupted us. Helen looked at it, inactive in shock. She must've switched it on whilst she was holding it. Drawing attention to itself, it rang ten, 15, 20 times. Snatching at it, our awkward companion took the initiative.

"Hello?" After nodding twice, he offered the phone to Helen. "It's Darren. For you, Jackie." Panicked, she mouthed silently her unavailability. He returned the mobile to his ear. "I'm sorry, she appears to be..."

"Indisposed," I prompted.

"Indisposed, but her friend Helen's here," he said. And passed the phone to me.

First published in *DWM* Issue 280, July 1999

A new life with Patrick in Leeds is calling – but Jackie still has some unfinished business with the Man in Black. Cue the flashback sequence...

Black Tuesday

At the time arranged, the dark figure of Darren Barry popped up from nowhere onto the horizon. His distant perspective allowed me to hold his approaching image between my thumb and forefinger – and, like Davros with his imaginary virus, snap them shut on him. It felt good.

We had gone to school together, singling each other out as villains. Between the ages of eight and 11 the energy we channelled into tormenting the other could have powered small cities. We were good enemies, the best of them, and worthy of the trouble we went to to prove it. At senior school, Claire had once said she thought I missed him, and that my catty relationship with Alison Stribling was a substitute. Whatever, Alison was a poor opponent. Gone were the grand threats and operatic gestures. The best she could muster were sarky comments on my hair, lack of blusher and musical taste. She'd cried off by the third year, when it became clear she'd be stuck with small tits.

Darren had stopped opposite; like a gunfighter in a western, he stood with ground between us. Arranged on our abandoned school playing field, this meeting was highly irregular. On prior occasions our paths had crossed by chance – the first being three years ago, over a decade since I'd last seen him. Flattered by the strength with which we recalled each other's childhood evil, the thin line between love and hate was breached. We'd matured only physically. The following morning had revealed our deviousness to be unchanged. The traps laid would've embarrassed a modern ten year-old – and I'd hoped he'd be equally pleased with those I'd set for him.

The second meeting was a little over a month ago, and initially something of a repeat performance. But its rushed conclusion had resulted in my acquiring Darren's mobile phone, mistaking it for my own. I'd now been asked to return it.

As ever, Darren was wearing black.

"The time has come to share your secret with me." Sometimes all he needed was the beard. "Tell me of Patrick."

"It was New Year's Eve," I began, "1997. Fancy dress. He was a Womble. Had to be Orinoco, didn't it? I mean, if it were Tomsk, no problem. I could resist Tomsk. And Tobermory – out of the question, for I hate moustaches. But Orinoco, everyone's favourite... I was drawn to him, he had an unfair advantage. I only knew it was Patrick when I looked under his snout. We had passed through each other's English groups at college. He was Laertes to my Ophelia. I spent my drowning drawing Daleks on his folder. He remembered, and started talking interestedly about *Doctor Who*. Not that I thought that was a come-on. But tanked up on Hooch, I misread his social kiss, causing me to return one that, over a year later, practically has me shacked up in Leeds with him.

"That wasn't the plan. The plan was for *Charlatan*, my BBC novel, to be accepted; for the insane plumbers Hubbub and Smutch to reappear in a sequel, and one where I would finally explore the concept of the Anti-Matter Moose. The plan was for Carol Smillie to turn and ask if I wouldn't mind standing in for her on future Lottery shows. The plan wasn't to be invited to a party at Patrick's parents' only to end up looking like a twig, searching Teletext for a duff Cannes report concerning a movie Doctor. Neither was it that his deaf and baffled Granny should draw to everyone's attention that I was a doctor, and that she'd have to be so loudly corrected over where her confusion arose. It wasn't the plan, when finding the Denys Fisher Tom Baker doll in a charity shop window, that research would reveal I'd purchased nothing more than a little Gareth Hunt.

"The plan was that when Nigel acquired a girlfriend, she'd be a witty and invigorating addition, and not Nicky Parrot, a glamour pustule with all the depth of a shallow soap dish. The plan was to like her, but I just wanted to feed her to pigeons, to see her run like Tippi Hedren in Hitchcock's *The Birds*. The plan was that when I'd eventually meet Tom Baker on his book-signing tour, my mouth would be able to articulate some kind of English instead of sounding like I would experience difficulty in counting to ten, or like something that had just been abandoned by the mother ship.

"The plan was that I would continue to sit round The Moon and Mushroom's circular tables, pairing Doctors to their most likely Spice Girl. That I would continue, with Chas and Nigel, to have absurd fan conversations, attributing, perhaps, a *Doctor Who* numeral to every one of its 36 years – (1) possibly being the number of real walls in a Troughton TARDIS, (2) the number of acceptable moments of CSO, (3) the amount of times the War Machine drew the expression "Fantastic!" from *Blue Peter*'s Christopher Trace without ever once sounding like he meant it, (4) from *The Mind Robber*, the curious collection of Polo mint bits that appear latterly at the corner of the Master's mouth, (5) the number of rejected faces from the Second Doctor's trial, at which point opinion would be canvassed about the third portrait offered being that of Dalek operator John Scott Martin. (6) would never be reached, for we would fall into discussion over Romana's *City of Death* comment concerning all Gallifreyan drawings being achieved by computer – concluding that, if this was in any way correct, then *The War Games* bunch must have been flogged some very dodgy software.

"It wasn't the plan, after our disagreement over my acquiring your mobile phone, that Helen and I would no longer laugh like spanners in her luckiest bar, nor that Nigel should inquire continually as to the identity of the mystery woman who kissed him at Claire's party. It wasn't the plan that I should meet you there. What happened at Claire's party was a mistake. I'm prone to mistakes. I'm good at them. Always do what you're best at, that's what I say. It isn't fair," I said. "I'm supposed to fill your mind. I'm supposed to torment you." Stopping, I took a calming breath and ran my fingers through my hair to tidy it. "Well, say something."

"When are you expected to be joining Patrick in Leeds?"

"At the end of the week," I answered. "But my letter would get there first. Would you believe the post office put a Dalek stamp on it?"

"Congratulations, Jackie – I always knew you'd do it."

"You did most of this – I was little more than a humble assistant." I withdrew two more letters from my coat pocket. "I've written some others that I'd need to send too."

"I've enjoyed my return home – I fly back tonight." He crossed to me. "The phone?" I retrieved it from my bag. "Forgive me for planting it there." Falling heavily on my mouth he allowed no response to this final revelation. "Remember – Flight 303. We can begin on a work permit as soon as I collect you."

I looked at the letters. To post them would start a chain of events. Even a humble assistant could do it.

First published in *DWM* Issue 350, December 2004

For several years, Jackie Jenkins has led a life of ordered calm, protected against all threats from ex-boyfriend Darren Barry by the Atlantic Ocean. Until...

October 1979

10am Junior school, queued up outside Mr Mills'.
"What's that?" I'm pointing at Claire's neck.
"A chain," she says, "and look..." she pulls at her collar, "a love-bite. What's that?" she asks back.
"*Doctor Who Weekly*. And look... transfers."

Jackie Jenkins – The Missing Years

Claire's been an odd friend. We drifted apart at secondary school, where she seemed to me to be in an unseemly rush to grow up. Our nine school years, however, mean we share a number of mutual friends. I always get a Christmas card, usually a lewd one, with a cone-like scribble at the bottom which I think is supposed to be a Dalek, and she always remembers me at parties.

Claire's parties were legend. They were the type where people actually danced and sang, and for years I had always enjoyed them. But this was to change, suddenly and terribly. It was at one of Claire's parties that I was to face one of the most dangerous crises in my short history. It was 1999, in the corner of one dark room, that my path once again crossed with Darren Barry's, my personal Man in Black. Darren was my junior school nemesis. Our days were spent thinking up ways we could torment each other. It was why we existed. I'd lay traps for him and he'd lay traps for me.

I'd nick his daps and he'd stuff my bag with grass and leaves. It was a peculiar kind of hate that bordered on mutual respect and even love. We were bound together in darkness. Our teachers always said we'd get ourselves into trouble, and that's what happened.

Claire's party had started a chain of events that shook the foundations of my universe to the very core, and ended up with me and Darren living in a small apartment in America. Chas would email often but never mention Darren. Nigel... well, apparently it was four weeks before he'd even realised I was gone. It was Nicky Parrot, a dreadful shallow ex of his, who had finally convinced Nigel that liking *Doctor Who* was not cool, and so, like Number Six, he had resigned and moved to a village. Giving up *Doctor Who* had also apparently meant giving up his friends – although I can hardly talk. Word that he'd been spotted recently with a Big Finish had sparked rumours that the new series had rekindled his interest. As it turned out, this was a big-boned Baltic woman and not a CD story at all. I had run into Nicky Parrot once since then as well. She was pregnant, and by a *Buffy* fan. Nicky clearly thought she had gone up in the world.

Anyway, the whole Darren/America thing lasted six months. Darren had stopped wearing black, but even in blue I couldn't trust him. That was the trouble with Darren – he was always looking for a new body.

October 2004

10pm Claire was having a good run of parties. This was the second in as many months and had the addition of being decked out in white fairy lights. Last time I got ill as a dog on something called Grappa and got dragged into some silly solo singing thing that was happening in the kitchen. Claire had just slayed them with her *Thank you for the music*. I went blank... well, almost.

"Klokeda, partha, mennin klatch, ablark, araan, aroon. Klokeeda shunna teerenatch, aroon, araan, aroon..."

True, no-one joined in on the chorus, but Claire's cat fell right off the top of the fridge.

The only problem with Claire, other than that she's a bit predatory, is she knows literally hundreds of people, and her parties seem to deal with them on rotas. I barely recognised any of this lot, save for the weird guy from her work who'd tried to throw a few shapes to my *Venusian Lullaby*. He looked to be making his way over so I tapped the shoulder of the girl next to me and started a conversation.

"Ah – how nice to see you again." This was rubbish, I didn't know her. Unfortunately she seemed to know me.

"Oh... it's Jenkins, isn't it?" She gave me a look as if I was bad news. "Didn't you disappear or something? Some scandal? That's it," she said. "You ran off with someone – someone from school."

"Oh, it's all been forgotten about now, you know."

"Oh really?" she said, sceptically.

"Mmm."

"So where have you been all these years?"

"Oh, here and there," I said. "You know, round and about."

"Canada, wasn't it?"

"No, no – America. Then a few months in Venice..."

"And wasn't there a boyfriend," she continued, "who never knew anything about it?" I decided I'd had enough of this line of questioning and feigned a wince. "Is there something the matter?"

"No, just a twinge in the knee." I rubbed at it through my jeans, adding it was probably the legacy of my rackety life. I changed the subject. "Remind me how you know Claire."

"She used to be at my work, Maximum Wattage. I put up the lights."

"Of course. And splendidly, if I may say so."

"Oh, do you think so?" My flattery was working.

"Oh yes – it's a gift," I beamed. "Somehow you've made the whole place come alive…"

11:15pm "What d'you think of Billie?" someone was asking. I knew what he meant, but it had been playing havoc with my conversations with Chas lately. Although, these days, it was Chas and Mike. Some people were surprised, but I knew… I knew right from the start.

"Gone are the days when Hartnell could just be plain 'Billy'," he'd said. "These days, a 'Billy' could be a 'Hartnell' or a 'Piper'." There was no problem on paper, of course – it was our verbal shorthand that was suffering.

I heard singing start up in the kitchen. Claire had come to fetch me, as she always wanted a full house for her performances, so I made my apologies and left the Billie fan saying that she'd be great and just as lovely as when he first bought her singles. I gave a casual glance over to my bag that I'd left in the hall, and that's when I saw it. It was stuffed with grass and leaves.

"What is it?" asked Claire.

"A sort of calling card," I said.

11:16pm Darren Barry was sitting at the top of the stairs. He had gone back to the black and was smiling.

"So you left America?" I said.

"Obviously."

"What about the bookshop girl?"

"What about her? You have always been my greatest stimulation."

"It won't work, Darren. We're a strictly 'once every four years' thing."

"And it's been four and a half," he replied. "You're a difficult girl to forget, Jackie. The things I read in the papers, what I see outside my window…" He was being enigmatic now, which he knew I liked, but he wasn't making much sense.

"New series," he purred. "Now I know you wouldn't be so shallow as to have any other motivation than to see me, but here's my address until Christmas." I took the folded piece of paper.

Cardiff.

The New Diaries

2005

Saturday 26 March

6:50pm (10 minutes before the broadcast of *Rose*) Please, please, please don't let this be shit...

Tuesday 31 May

11:30am (somewhere on the A23) Chas, James and myself had decided to visit the new *Doctor Who* Exhibition situated on Brighton Pier.

"We should go while the show's still on air and there's still a buzz about it," Chas had said.

The only problem with this was that the exhibition had only opened a couple of weeks ago and as its organisers had said it would only be putting exhibits in after they had appeared on television, nobody wanted to go all that way and end up not seeing very much.

As Brighton's sea popped up on the horizon, we all congratulated ourselves on how we thought we'd got the timing of our visit just right. The truth, however, was that our enthusiasm had simply got the better of us. Steven Moffat's episodes *The Empty Child* and *The Doctor Dances* had been popular with all of us, particularly James, who wasn't even a fan in the true sense of the word but who had heard Radio 1's Chris Moyles raving about the episodes and had taken from that that the show had somehow gained some extra level of approval. Even so, it was clear that the episodes didn't offer much in the way of exhibits bar perhaps a model of the gas-masked empty child itself, but buoyed up by our own conversations we couldn't wait any longer.

My reaction to the return of *Doctor Who* has gone through several stages. Following the initial surprise that something was actually going to happen, I quickly became rather distant and ambivalent about it. It was an act of preservation, of course, one mainly designed to stave off too much disappointment if it all went pear-shaped. Nevertheless, it was an act that quickly became a weird kind of truth. I found it incredibly easy not to go online or scour the newspapers for gossip. Chas couldn't understand it. Sometimes he'd be absolutely bursting with rumour, but I decided to stick with *DWM* on this and trust their judgement over what information I should know.

Some news, of course, is just too big to avoid. I was on holiday in Paris when I got a text from Chas: "Christopher Eccleston is new Who." I sat in some weak sunlight looking at the words and not feeling at all sure about the choice. For a while I even hoped it wasn't true. That afternoon I found a sprawling Virgin Megastore and walked around it, not really concentrating.

I found out about Billie Piper's casting in a newsagent's, seeing it emblazoned on the front of *The Daily Mail*: "*Doctor Who* girl is pop star Billie..." or something along those lines. I wasn't too positive about that either – it just felt gimmicky.

Chas became completely irate at the news that the Daleks may not be in the new series due to some legal wrangles with Terry Nation's Estate.

"What an idiot," he said, as if Nation was still alive and personally responsible. "Where are the Daleks going to appear if not in *Doctor Who*? As the new family in *EastEnders*?"

I just thought how disappointed people would be.

My slight irritation with the show hovered about me until just before last Christmas. The turning point came when a work colleague waddled over to me with a picture from that day's *Sun*.

"Seen this?" he said, chewing on the end of a sandwich.

By this time the Dalek problem had been ironed out, and they were back in the show. I took the paper from him, already folded at the appropriate page, and there it was. A new series Dalek. Gold. Chunky. Beautiful. I asked if I could have the picture and at home put it on a big 'to file' pile in the spare room. The thing seemed to have some sort of magnetic draw on me. I must have looked at it about 15 times that night. The last time I mooned over a picture that much it was a *Robin of Sherwood* Michael Praed back in 1984.

In early March I went on a short break to Venice with Helen. We'd sit in a bar just off St Mark's Square – La Principessa – where, behind large bug-eyed sunglasses, Helen would rate all the men that went by. The categories were simple: 'hot', 'fit' and 'very fit'. In the evening we'd go to the Octopus Bar, a kind of jazz café that stayed open 'til three, which I'd discovered on my last visit. Helen met Marco. He was from Birkenhead.

The timing of our break was significant. The BBC was being coy about when the new series was going to start but the hot money was on the Easter weekend. My enthusiasm for the show was now where it should be. Eccleston and Piper looked good and there was no way I was going to chance missing it.

Back home, I watched Russell T Davies' *Casanova*. *Doctor Who*'s new lead writer and Venice meant it was a must-see. I loved it. So did Chas. Nobody had made a connection between Russell T Davies and Christopher Eccleston, despite Eccleston playing the lead in Davies' modern-day 'Son of God' drama *The Second Coming*. This time neither Chas nor myself were quite so slow on the uptake. Both of us recognised a certain cheeky charisma in David Tennant's Casanova. Even Helen liked it and from nowhere, Tennant had rocketed into a strong position in her list of 'Most fanciable men'.

The first episode of the new series went out and my first thought about it was that it was '*Doctor Who*-lite'. Chas came round afterwards and we swapped positive comments on the leads, the titles, the music and the sheer pace of the thing, but there was an underlying feeling that the story wasn't up to much. Chas said it was like watching the last episode of an old series four-parter.

"We joined the story as it was already happening," he said, "so there was no beginning and middle, just an end."

It took me a few viewings before I realised that that was the brilliance of it. By my fourth watch, I had Rose's freeze-framed, last-minute dash to the TARDIS down as one of the series' most joyous moments ever.

Chas went mental when the news broke that Eccleston was quitting the series, although his concern was more to do with how the general public might react.

"We've already had one episode and it's already going wrong," he said.

If Eccleston's quick departure was the most surprising news of the day, the choice of David Tennant as the man tipped to replace him was the most obvious.

1.30pm (Brighton Pier) We eat lunch to the sound of James talking about *Quadrophenia*. He was convinced the concrete arch to the cafe where we were sitting had featured in the film, and every now and then, he would burst into a tad-too-loud chorus of "We are, we are, we are the Mods…"

"Like a bit of Who then, do you?" said the waitress, as we paid her.

This made me laugh, almost as much as the time somebody interrupted Chas reminiscing about the first time he saw *Genesis*.

"Were you at the Roundhouse?" the man asked.

"No," Chas said, "I was at my Nan's…"

The exhibition was signposted by a Police Box prop placed at the foot of the pier, which was surrounded by people posing for photographs. Chas' fear that Eccleston's departure might damage public interest had been unfounded. If anything, all the speculation around it had kept the series' profile high. The latest news was that Moffat's episodes had just been cut to make them less scary.

The exhibition was in a domed building bang in the middle of the pier and in front of an Arcade Emporium and a completely barmy-looking rollercoaster called Crazy Mouse. Inside it was a large space and, as we thought, just that little bit too big for the limited number of costumes and props on display.

"They'll have to change that," said James, craning his neck up at a huge canvas of Eccleston and Piper. Tennant had been confirmed as Doctor Ten just a matter of weeks ago. It felt odd to feel already used to him. I'd been around long enough to see six new actors take on the role and none of them seemed so instantly right as this. There was the age issue, of course. For the first time, I was facing the prospect of a Doctor younger than myself, albeit not by much. There was a vague worry that this was going to be a watershed moment. Like with *Blue Peter* in the late Eighties. I could take Lesley Judd saying "I bet you don't know what this is made of," at the top of some *Blue Peter* 'make' but definitely not Yvette Fielding. From my perspective, she was just a girl.

One of the things that's been strange getting used to about the new series is how fast news about it travels. Back in the Eighties, news came in monthly doses from the pages of *DWM*. By the mid-Nineties there was the Net, but with the show off-air, most of this news seemed to revolve around which stories were going to be released on BBC Video. In 2000 the whole process started again, but this time with DVD.

These were lean times.

Now there's *Doctor Who* news everywhere. Over the last nine weeks the series has been given the same level of press attention as *EastEnders*. Three episodes in, I discovered you could go online to find the overnight figures of the previous episode. This action has become part of a new Sunday morning routine and I'm annoyed by how much my stomach churns when doing it and, when the figures aren't quite as good as the previous week's, by how much it affects my own view of a story. I had got used to people ignoring *Doctor Who* and now they were interested again, every fluctuation in the figures seemed to carry an extra significance. What was it about one story that didn't make them want to watch the next one? Despite Chris Moyles' praise, the figures for Moffat's episodes were down on the rest of the series.

The first part of the exhibition showcased a collection of classic series monsters. Further down, the Doctor and Rose's costumes spun slowly on a revolving dais, and around the corner stood three Auton brides and The Face of Boe. The exhibition had gone heavy on behind-the-scenes material, with many 'press button' displays illuminating subjects such as set design and special effects. The best exhibit was a new series Dalek which had been raised at an angle to give the impression it was hovering. We all took about a dozen photographs before we were nudged out of the way by some excited nine year-olds. They were in awe of it. It was their first Dalek and they whacked the button that made it talk over and over again.

We left the exhibition with a plan to see the Brighton Pavilion, look about the town and find a curry house. James wimped out and chose something mild. I chose something that sounded like a 'Thal' because, well, it had been that kind of day.

We got back to the car later than planned and made ourselves later again when we remembered it was *Radio*

Times day, and stopped off at a service station to buy one and read what it said about next Saturday's episode, *Boomtown*. James bought a bag of Doritos. We got back to the car full of *Doctor Who* thoughts. Chas flicked on the radio. It was Fat Boy Slim, *Praise you*. First line: "We've come a long, long way together, through the bad times and the good…"

It seemed apt for this day, and for a while now, quite a few others.

2006

Wednesday 20 September

One of the strangest things about the success of the new *Doctor Who* is how my love for it has made me quite critical of the old. This isn't to do with the way the series looks. Any comparisons along those lines would be pointless. My issue is with the series' storytelling style. The most obvious difference is the emotional wallop the new series carries. Not everyone likes it – and I can understand that. A number of Virgin's *New Adventures* novels did this sort of thing and I never liked it there. But *Father's Day* was a completely different *Doctor Who* experience. I cried watching it and from there on, the show seemed to be operating on a different level.

In *The Parting of the Ways,* when the hologram of Eccleston's Doctor turns to Rose and asks her to promise him that she'll have a "fantastic life", the power of that scene literally took my breath away. At the end of the episode, Vortex Rose comes back to save the day and the crack in Piper's voice when she says "I want you safe...my Doctor" never fails to put a lump in my throat. It's the same for the end of *School Reunion*, and the last sad scenes of *The Girl in the Fireplace*.

Since 2005, I have so much new material to look at that I find I watch the old series less than I used to. But when I do, it's this emotional level that I miss the most. When the old series gears itself up for a sad scene – usually at the departure of a companion or Doctor – it suddenly loses all its usual bravado and comes across like an awkward teenager not knowing what to do or say. Some see this as part of the series' character and charm, but following Rose's utter despair at the loss of her Doctor in *The Christmas Invasion* and *Doomsday*'s Bad Wolf Bay scene, it just looks like the programme playing safe and ignoring what has proved to be an exceptionally rich vein of material.

Another thing that impresses me is how well the new series handles the programme's huge history. When I first heard that Sarah Jane and K9 were coming back in Series Two, I thought it was just a joke or fan rumour. I couldn't understand why, following such a bold and successful revival, the show would want to bring back two characters from the past. Surely this was just empty nostalgia. A repeat of one of the mistakes of the 1980s. *School Reunion*, however, completely floored me. How had this story never been done? The original series ran for 26 years, long enough for something like it. All it took was initiative. Of course Sarah Jane loved the Doctor. Of course her life was never the same again. Of course there would be jealousy between the new girl and the ex. The old show only pushed companions together for anniversary specials, where they all behaved towards each other like they were members of a Gentleman's Club. Rose's shock at learning she was just the latest in a long line did more to convey the Doctor's great age and past than a hundred flashback sequences.

The Time War and the destruction of Gallifrey is also genius. The Daleks were the Doctor's greatest enemy because kids liked them and the show kept bringing them back. Making the Daleks the survivors of a war that killed the Time Lords and made the Doctor the last of his race completely raises the game. Stick that behind even the weakest old series Dalek story and suddenly the whole thing's got extra resonance.

I'm also surprised by how quickly I've let go of ideas that I thought would be sacrosanct. I no longer really want stories told over four or six episodes. You go onto chat rooms and you find people complaining that the fast pace of the show means there's no room to explore character. Back in the old days, though, the criticism would be different and long stories were often slated for padding. Most fans would agree that even the third episode of a four-parter would be where you find a sub-plot. To be honest, I don't really agree with the argument in the first place. Can you really say the show has no room for characterisation after an episode like *Father's Day*, or that we didn't get to know Madame de Pompadour in *The Girl in the Fireplace*? The series under Russell T Davies has a knack for succinctness. We learn more about Sarah Jane Smith in *School Reunion* than we do from her original run of stories, and has there ever been a more touching portrayal of ordinariness than *Love and Monsters*' Elton Pope?

I never thought I'd give up the idea of the inside of the TARDIS being anything other than a gleaming white control room. I thought I'd fight any move to change it all the way. But as soon as I saw the new series version, I fell in love with it immediately. I love the unearthly glow of it and the approach to the console as a mix of Time Lord technology and junk shop chic. Some say steampunk has been done to death but not in *Doctor Who*, and I can't think of a character or show that suits it better.

The other day someone asked me who my favourite companion was, and at this moment it's Rose, because of the way she was written, because of the journey she's been on, because she so clearly loves the Doctor and because of Piper's playing of her. She's toppled Elisabeth Sladen as Sarah Jane Smith and it's odd how guilty I feel about that. They're only TV characters, after all. The writing is on the wall though, I fear. I finished Series One thinking it was the most perfectly formed series ever. Tom Baker's my favourite Doctor and, with seven years of stories to his name, I think that's going to hold true for a while yet. But it's strange how any possible change in that situation worries me.

2007

Monday 25 June

I hadn't seen party girl Claire for some time and then, just a few days ago, bumped into her outside HMV, me holding a copy of *Salem's Lot*, her a bag from some expensive-looking clothes shop. She was with a friend, Naomi, whose dark curls and olive-skinned attractiveness would've been annoying if she hadn't been so warm and friendly.

We'd been chatting for about 30 minutes when Claire suggested we should go for a drink and soon we were all sitting round a high table, sharing a bottle of wine and picking at a huge slice of chocolate cake with three separate forks. Most of the conversation consisted of Claire telling Naomi what I was like at school.

"Remember when you came back from half-term and you'd had your hair flicked back like that girl from *Charlie's Angels*?"

"Love *Charlie's Angels*," said Naomi.

"Favourite?" I asked.

"Sabrina Duncan."

"Good choice."

"Of course, Jackie's all *Doctor Who* these days," interrupted Claire.

"Love *Doctor Who*," said Naomi. I glanced at Claire. She hadn't been expecting this. She had mentioned *Doctor Who* because she thought it was still an untrendy thing and she was hoping to embarrass me. "Did you see the one in the school where the Doctor made himself human?"

"Yes, brilliant story."

"Oh, it was so sad," she said. "And The Face of Boe...they've killed The Face of Boe." She made a weepy face to show she thought this sad too.

I still find it strange hearing people talk about *Doctor Who*. Chas loves it. He's always reporting conversations overheard on the train or at work.

"It's just like the Seventies," he says. "It's back on top."

It's different for me though. Bar watching it as a kid, my passion for the series grew in the mid-Eighties, when the audience was shrinking and it appeared as if no-one was talking about it at all. *Doctor Who* was something discussed with close friends and other fans. It wasn't a topic for the pub or office, and it certainly wasn't something many women talked about.

Naomi's conversation bounced onto something else, and I was happy to let it go. This is something I've discovered about myself recently. Since the show's come back, I'm much more relaxed about this kind of thing. I don't feel the need to stir peoples' interest in it or engineer a conversation round to mention it. I'm happy to hear that they are enjoying it and to leave it at that. The show itself is carrying the message now. It doesn't need me to instigate conversations about favourite Doctors or whether anyone remembers 'the one with the maggots'. People are wary of obsessives anyway, and I wouldn't want to put anyone off it by coming over all geeky.

Doctor Who is cool these days and one of the best things about being a fan right now is that you can be cool about it too. An average audience of seven to eight million watched Series Three so, so what if you overhear a negative comment or read a nasty review online? The majority of the audience aren't reading message boards anyway.

After Series One I went from the weird girl at work with the Dalek calendar to someone who was lending out DVDs to colleagues who were suddenly interested in seeing "some of the old ones". Most of them were disappointed, finding them slow, but rather than bang on about why I liked them, I simply let them get back to enjoying the new.

"Refill, Jackie?" Claire was gesturing to me with the wine bottle. I pushed my glass forward.

"OK, share it out." Naomi pushed hers forward too.

"I found an old photograph of us the other day," Claire said. "A school one, with all of us lined up on the grass."

I knew exactly the one she meant. We all had one. Junior School 1978, outside Mr Mills'. My Mum had put it in a frame and it had sat on top of the family telly, yellowing slightly, well into the late Eighties. Claire was at the back, standing and wearing a pink and white striped cardy that always reminded me of Bagpuss. I was middle row, perched on a chair, in a burgundy tunic thing with white socks that came up to the knee. In front of me and sitting cross-legged on the grass was my playground nemesis, Darren Barry, in black jumper and cords. My smile was more of a grimace as, just at the point the picture was taken, Darren had pinched me hard on the back of the leg. I got him back when I filled his duffle coat pockets with mashed potato, smuggled out of the canteen.

"Who's that girl with all the ringlets and the cat T-shirt?" asked Claire.

"Tessa someone," I said. "I can't remember her surname."

I knew where the conversation was going, of course. She was going to ask me about Darren. I looked at Naomi, wondering if she knew the story. Claire was a gossip at school, and she was a gossip now. Had she already been told about me and Darren? About how we were best enemies at school and how later we had become something quite different. Something much more adult and complicated. Claire had always been fascinated with our on/off relationship. When Darren had convinced me to go to America with him and it had all gone wrong on my discovery of the bookshop girl, it was Claire who was one of the first to contact me, to see how I was and to immerse herself in another instalment.

Claire took a sip of her wine and, turning to Naomi, blurted it all out.

"Jackie went out with a boy in our class. Not then but later. They moved to the States and everything."

"It didn't work out," I said, in the most casual voice I could muster. "Big mistake. I shouldn't have done it."

"What was he like?" asked Naomi. I smiled slightly at the thought of him.

"You know in the last series of *Doctor Who*, when the Doctor met his old enemy the Master? I've always thought of him like that, but without the Prime Minister bit and the glam wife."

It was at that point that Claire leaned forward, her face bursting with news.

"Haven't you heard? Darren's got married."

Tuesday 3 July

6pm The thing I was dreading most popped into my email with a cheery "Hiya". It was Claire. Despite her upbeat tone, I read the message with the sound of the TARDIS' Cloister Bell ringing in my head. Impending disaster. Man the lifeboats.

"How's you?" it read. "Great to catch up the other day. It's been ages! How you fixed for Saturday? I'm going out with a small group of friends and I thought it would be great if you can come along too. Naomi's coming. She thought you were great btw. Thought we'd try that new super-pub – you know, the one that used to be the old auction rooms. What d'you think?"

It's been just over a week since Claire told me about Darren and the thought of it has practically invaded my brain ever since. I watched ten minutes of *Salem's Lot* and switched it off, finding it impossible to concentrate. The news of it felt like a steel blade being thrust into my gut and

I was furious by how angry it had made me. I stood in front of the mirror practising retorts I might have with him. I borrowed from everywhere, but the only one that really captured how I felt was Avon's from the last episode of *Blake's 7*:

"You...? Betrayed me?"

The thing I dreaded about Claire's email was how it was so absolutely and typically her. When she told me about Darren, and I asked how she had come to hear about it, I thought even then, I bet she'll try and contrive some situation to get the two of us together. I had long suspected the way we kept crossing paths at Claire's parties was more than coincidence, and it was a reason why, in the last few years, I had started to find excuses for not attending.

For Claire to hold another party would have been obvious, but an invitation to a few drinks in a bar sounded more casual. More on the hoof. I could just imagine how it would go. It would all be fairly light and silly until, halfway through the evening, a shadow would fall over me and there he would be. Darren Barry. Somehow miraculously back in town. Dressed in black and presenting me with his trophy wife. His cruellest trick yet.

The most sensible thing to do with this invitation was to turn it down. If it was a trap then I was pretty sure no good would come of it. But Claire had dropped an absolute bombshell when she mentioned Darren's wife, and to say I was curious about what she was like was a massive understatement. If I went along I'd find out, or, if by any coincidence Darren turned up alone, at least he'd have pictures on his phone or something.

8pm I decide I'm going to go. If I don't, the curiosity will eat me up from the inside. I decide I'm going to play it all flippant and *City of Death*. A scenario pops into my head:

"Oh, so you're Darren's wife? You're a very beautiful woman...probably."

And then another, bang up-to-date this time. I could wait until she pops to the loo or something and then corner her, like the *Sunday Times* woman does to Lucy Saxon in *The Sound of Drums*:

"I have reason to believe you're in very great danger. Not just you but myself as well, in fact. Your husband is not who he says he is. I'm sorry, but it's a lie. Everything's a lie. All of it. The school days, the degree, the business trips...it's all invented."

I'll email Claire tomorrow, all bright and breezy.

9pm Second thoughts. Why should I put myself through it? I can't imagine anything more awkward and hateful. I'll email Claire tomorrow, saying I already have something planned for Saturday.

10pm Vworp vworp. The TARDIS materialisation sound effect I put on my mobile phone to amuse myself goes off. It's a text. No name, just a long number I don't recognise. I press 'view'.

"It's been a long time," it says. "Looking forward to seeing you Saturday. D."

10.35pm (One Smirnoff Ice later, glugged down at an unseemly rate) The text was confirmation. Claire *had* been up to her old tricks. I had worked it out, and I'm sure when she had contacted Darren with a similar invitation, so had he. It wouldn't have taken much for him to get my new number out of her. In fact, when she realised she'd lost the element of surprise, I suspect she volunteered it in the hope the situation would snowball naturally. I clicked the text up for about the fiftieth time.

I thought it was good of Darren to take away any doubt over the situation. I liked him for that. My finger wavered over the 'reply' key. I pressed it.

"Hi," I typed, and after an even longer hesitation, hit the 'send'.

10.46pm Vworp vworp. "Hi."
Reply: "So…married then?"

10.48pm Vworp vworp. "I know. It's good, isn't it?"
Reply: "Where did you meet?"

10.50pm Vworp vworp. "Cardiff Station – waiting for you…"
Reply: "That's ironic."

10.51pm Vworp vworp. "I thought so."

The last contact I had with Darren was through a text. The last time we met, he told me that his job had taken him to Cardiff and he was using the fact that the new series of *Doctor Who* was being filmed there as bait to get me to visit. He called several times, each invite laced with the same temptation.

Around December 2004, I crumbled. But at the station, had a change of heart and stood back as my train went by. The overnight bag said it all. I texted when I got home:

"Sorry Darren. Bad idea, I think."

10.53pm Vworp vworp. "Still there?"
Reply: "Yes. What's she like?"

10.54pm Vworp vworp. " :-) "
Reply: "Not sure if Saturday's a good idea. Best we leave it, don't you think?"

10.55pm Vworp vworp. " :-("
Reply: "Honestly? Claire's going to make a meal of it, whatever happens. Why give her the satisfaction?"

10.58pm Vworp vworp. "The arrangement's for nine. Why don't I get there earlier? Same place. How about seven?"
Reply: "Just you, or…"

11pm Vworp vworp. "Just me."

Saturday 7 July

6.55pm The old auction rooms were grand and the super-pub that had taken their place was equally palatial. I could see Darren. He was outside, leaning against a rail of a terrace area that had been situated at the top of some broad marble steps. Being summer, people were in light clothes, but not Darren, who stood out in his usual trademark black. He looked thinner, older. How did I appear to him, I thought? The same? Worse? He was by a table, with a bottle of wine and two glasses of red already poured. He handed one to me and I saw his wedding ring. I had planned to be nonchalant but the sight of it made me feel hostile. Darren caught my gaze.

"Ah yes," he said, turning the ring with his thumb. "One year, three months."

"Well, I hope you're good to her," I said, forcing out a laugh. "I mean, does she know what you're like? I mean, there's definitely got to be no bookshop girl. Definitely no bookshop girl. And definitely no, no…"

"No you?"

"Definitely no me. I mean, definitely no me. Certainly no me." I laughed again, a nervous one, the kind you do when you think someone's caught you out. "I mean, that's just not going to happen. Certainly not now you're...you know. With the ring and everything."

"It does come off, you know." He drew it from his finger and rolled it about in his other hand.

"You can put that right back on," I said.

Darren was joking with me, but I knew him. In a year or two, this wouldn't be a joke, it would be something dangerous and unkind, and I suddenly felt exhausted by him – by the both of us, in fact.

I drank my wine and chatted about a few useless bits and pieces from work. Darren even asked me what I thought about the new series, although he made it clear that he never watched it. It was then that I realised what I really needed to say. I had been going over quotes and put-downs I could use to get me through this evening, but nothing seemed to fit right now. Then suddenly, from nowhere, something popped into my head. The best one I could ever use. It would need tweaking a bit, of course, but it was completely brilliant, and what's more, only a couple of weeks old.

"I'm gonna go now," I said. "Give my apologies to the others. Or better still, don't even say I was here. You see, it's like my friend. She loved this bloke, and all he ever did was mess her around. She wasted years pining after him. Because while he was around, she never looked at anyone else. And I told her, get out. So Darren, my old friend, this is me...getting out. Thanks for the wine."

I turned, walked down the steps and didn't look back.

Whoever heard of anyone having a nemesis called Darren anyway? Let alone a lover.

2008

Tuesday 1 July

The world's gone *Doctor Who* mad at the moment. I didn't think it could get any better than 2005 but then Tennant happened and suddenly every woman in the office is a dyed-in-the-wool fan. On Saturday, *The Stolen Earth* ended with what seemed like the Doctor starting to regenerate. Monday morning, work was a-buzz with it. If Tennant wasn't already everyone's favourite Doctor, then the suggestion he was leaving, and so quickly and unannounced, had practically canonised him.

My reaction to *The Stolen Earth*'s cliffhanger was to revel in its audacity. But by the time the words 'To be continued' thundered onto the screen, I was fairly sure it was all a bluff. Tennant had been seen filming the Christmas Special, after all. The only way round that would be if he was filming a flashback sequence.

Being a *Doctor Who* fan sometimes seems to be all about having favourites. Favourite Doctor. Favourite companion. Favourite story. Favourite writer. Favourite monster. Favourite series. Favourite TARDIS landing. You name it. If you're a *Morse* fan, you can't have a favourite Morse, or Lewis, because they're all John Thaw and Kevin Whately. You can't have a favourite writer because they're all Colin Dexter (well, the *Morse*s were, anyway). You can't have a favourite Kirk or Spock because they're all William Shatner and Leonard Nimoy. You can have a favourite James Bond and *Bond* film, but the two don't necessarily have to tie up (*On Her Majesty's Secret Service*/Roger Moore). And you can have a favourite Sherlock Holmes, but in that case practically everyone's had a go, so you end up honing it down to just Rathbone or Brett.

Having a favourite Doctor is an essential part about being a fan. People ask you about it and if you don't have a definitive answer, you don't really sound like you know what you're talking about. Balanced answers are just no good. I remember being at a convention once where someone asked quite a well-known fan who their favourite Doctor was, and he said it was a bit like asking a father to pick his favourite son – they've all got their individual qualities. For a while I thought this answer was brilliant, all fair and diplomatic. But of course it just isn't true – not in Doctors or families. One is going to suit you more than the other. One is going to be best. It's tough but that's the way it is.

My favourite Doctor is Tom Baker. It's been like that practically forever. It's always nice if you like the Doctor of the moment, and to some degree I always have, but none of them have ever posed any serious threat to the Number One. The other day, somebody asked me who my favourite Doctor was, and for the first time since I can really remember, my answer suddenly didn't seem to sound so definite. I wanted to add another bit on the end. Another name. But didn't, because it just felt wrong. Disloyal. Weak. The truth is, David Tennant's becoming a bit of a problem. Not to the series, but to my world order.

It wasn't always like this. In 2006 I found parts of Tennant's performance a little too 'eager to please'. Eccleston played the part with a fair amount of suppressed anger. Most of the time he looked like a silver-backed gorilla who's being forced to walk up and down his cage. In contrast, Tennant's grinny, happy-go-lucky persona could be irritating. When he pretended to be drunk in the otherwise excellent *The Girl in the Fireplace*, I remember feeling a bit embarrassed by it – like his burst of Ray Parker Junior's *Ghostbusters* in *Army of Ghosts*, these instances seem to hint at excesses that might come even more to the fore once he had settled into the role. The change comes with Rose's departure. Russell T Davies' series is a smiling, optimistic thing as far as the human race is concerned, but I think his Doctors are best a little bit miserable. *The Runaway Bride* ends with the Doctor rejected and teary-eyed at the thought of travelling alone. In *Gridlock* he's at it again, welling up, remembering Gallifrey before it was destroyed. Tennant's performance in this makes me as upset as the Doctor. It's even worse than Rose's farewell because there the Doctor's trying to be brave about things. He even seems to be working from a roughly prepared speech, where in *Gridlock* it seems to bubble up from nowhere, all raw and unplanned.

Chas won't have anything to do with this line of thinking. Tom's his favourite Doctor and has been since halfway through *Genesis of the Daleks*. But Chas is older. He watched the Third Doctor regenerate when *Planet of the Spiders* was first broadcast in 1974. He was there at the start and his loyalty was reinforced, week in week out, over seven years.

Tennant's the most popular Doctor at work because most of the women there fancy him, and he's the one who's on TV at the moment. I had a Character Options figure of him on my desk for a while. The reaction bordered on the ridiculous. Women literally cooed over it.

"Wish it was the real thing," said one.

It actually went missing for a while, and then turned up again, its limbs slightly pulled about. I haven't really been sure about it since.

At the beginning of the year, I went to see three new comedians. The middle one – a woman in her late twenties – had worked up a whole routine about Tennant and what she'd do to him in bed. Most of the audience seemed to lap it up. I sat there confused, half-delighted the show had such a popular leading man and half-concerned as to whether anyone in the room was watching for the right reason.

What's captured my imagination about the Tenth Doctor's run of stories is how they strive to do different things with the character. All of the Doctors offer variety in terms of the stories they're in, but how the Doctor as the hero is used remains pretty much the same. Tom Baker used to annoy fans when he said the Doctor wasn't an acting part. He meant that the role never developed – the Doctor never fell in love, got married or had kids. Baker's solution was to keep audiences interested by making the Doctor unpredictable, but he still started one story in much the same way he started the next. The Tenth Doctor has done all of these things, in a roundabout sort of a way. He's fallen in love with Rose and Reinette, and suffered for losing them both. In *Human Nature*, we see him in human form, married and with kids, and in *The Doctor's Daughter*, with a daughter he's struggling to educate and look after. The Tenth Doctor is clever-dick Time Lord one week and something completely different the next. What's more, he doesn't forget what's happened to him by the start of the next adventure. The stories have repercussions. Events linger on. And he learns from them.

Human Nature is a standout story. When it was first shown I thought it was my favourite story ever. Tennant is brilliant as the human John Smith, awkwardly romancing school nurse Joan Redfern, and many have said how they couldn't imagine any of the other Doctors doing this so well. I don't know about that. Tennant's Doctor is a more human Doctor, and I can see other 'human' Doctors, such as Davison and McGann, working well in that situation too. What's more to the point is that they never had the chance. The Tenth Doctor has had scripts that make some of the other Doctors' rushing about look shallow and played out.

Tom Baker *is* my favourite Doctor but he was brilliant in a narrower field of material. Stories where the Doctor was always the Doctor. *The Invasion of Time* tries to step outside this and present the Doctor as a villain and a traitor to the Time Lords, but it isn't a particularly well-honed script and Baker's not at his best. Perhaps it is difficult to imagine Baker in *Human Nature*, but I can definitely see him in the brilliant *Midnight*, particularly early on. Imagine *The Robots of*

Death's Sandminer crew and the *Midnight* creature driving them half demented.

Of course, new *Doctor Who* is just that – new and still shiny, and I'm sure I'll feel different about it as time goes on. I remember being excited by the 'more than just a Time Lord' stuff of the Seventh Doctor, but now that part of it just comes across a bit confused and half-baked. The important thing about my awkward *ménage a trois* is what happens now. Does Tennant stay on after next year's Specials to be even more impressive or does it all come crashing down with a duff run of stories? Perhaps it's Jon Pertwee I should feel sorry for. Third place. And I don't even feel comfortable with that...

2010

Saturday 26 June

6pm (Glastonbury Festival) Big day. *Doctor Who*'s on and I'm not watching it. Instead, I'm a quarter of the way back from the Pyramid Stage, moving my hips in a weird figure-of-eight formation in front of Colombian temptress Shakira. It's an absolutely baking hot day. The straw hat I bought is proving completely ineffectual as any kind of visor and my shoulders are starting to burn pink.

It's not just any episode. It's the last episode of Series Five. The finale, as they like to call it these days. *The Big Bang*. And I'm putting all my trust in that my Sony hard disk recorder is going to click on at the right time, and that all the other Glastonbury highlight shows I've also pre-programmed to record aren't somehow going to upset its brains.

I blame *Doctor Who*'s 'gap year' for this. In 2008 I finally summoned up the courage to book for Glastonbury. It looked huge fun but all the people, those crowds and the possibility of bad weather... Yes, courage was the right word.

2009's event was book-ended by two heavy downpours, but held onto some sunny weather in the middle. I was struck by the friendliness of it all, and how moving it can be when a crowd all sing and dance in unison. Tom Jones belted out *Green Green Grass of Home* and I burst into tears. Same again when Blur closed Sunday night with an anthemic version of *Tender*. *Doctor Who* should've been on. But BBC Wales' decision to miss a year and just make four Specials meant that it wasn't. I wasn't missing anything. I was free.

I booked up for Glastonbury 2010 as soon as the tickets went online. So here I am, watching Shakira twist and twirl herself about while *Doctor Who*, all invisible and high above my head, is making its way into homes and TVs.

I'm not the type to miss episodes. Never have. In the Eighties people would say "But you're recording it, aren't you?" and I would say "Yeah, but you've still got to be there to work the video. You don't leave anything as important as that to a timer – or worse, a parent." Technology now means you can catch up on an episode in any number of ways, but to me that's not really the point. The best way to watch *Doctor Who* is as it always was – live, and as a shared experience. I mean, look at this year's viewing figures. They're all over the place because of this 'time-shift' business of people watching it when it suits them. Who wants to watch an episode four days after everybody else, when any surprises it may hold have already been discussed, or in the press? It's certainly not a viable option for fans.

From 2005 to the end of Series Four, I had seen all of the new series episodes on first transmission. Crunch time came with the 2009 Specials. *The Waters of Mars* was suddenly scheduled on a Sunday, clashing with a theatre gig by stand-up comedian Stewart Lee that I had already bought tickets for. I decided to be adult about it. My hard disk recorder had only messed up once, when a thunderstorm had broken transmission, and tonight was a clear night. By the time Stewart Lee would be on, the story would already be halfway through. No point worrying about it then. I could watch it all in my own time when I got back.

In the interval, a woman turns on her phone.

"Hi – everything OK?" She seemed to be talking to someone young. "What was *Doctor Who* like? Really? She shoots herself? Yeah, I know the Ood – the ones with the spaghetti faces. Sounds good. Is Dad there?"

Thanks for that, I thought.

8.15pm (Pyramid Stage) The Scissor Sisters aren't exactly the best band to be easing my present thoughts and worries. Series Three's *The Last of the Time Lords* used the track *I can't decide* off of their second album *Ta-dah*, and the worst kept secret of the weekend is that *Voyage of the Damned* guest-star Kylie Minogue is going to make a surprise appearance and sing with them.

I curse the weather. Not because I don't want to be burnt but because I know had bad all this sunshine's going to hit the ratings. I've always been obsessed with viewing figures but ever since a mini-heatwave wiped out the audience for Eccleston's swansong *The Parting of the Ways*, I've become equally fanatical about the weather. I start watching forecasts on Thursday, looking for rain or a general dullness that might keep people in round about six o'clock Saturday. If there's one thing that's dented my enjoyment of the series since 2005, it's having to pull the curtains on a sunny spring or summer day just so I can see the bloody screen. It just doesn't seem right – watching *The Impossible Planet* with the smell of next door's barbecue smoking its way into the house. Yet what's the alternative? Autumn, but with Simon Cowell and *The X Factor* stamping all over it. *Britain's Got Talent*'s bad enough – see the impact that's had. *Doctor Who*'s gone from seven to six just to avoid the potential of losing out to a dancing dog or a nutty Granny in a rah-rah skirt.

The Glastonbury rumour mill proves 100% accurate. Kylie takes to the stage. The crowd erupts.

"I love her," says a woman next to me. "I really love her."

I look at my watch. Well over by now, I think. Even BBC Three's *Confidential*. Wonder if there've been any revelations about River Song?

Joe catches my glance and puts an arm round me.

"Don't worry," he says. "Everything'll be alright. Promise."

Series Five has been a funny one for me. I had got used to feeling supremely confident about the series and I haven't felt like that as much this year. Me and Chas have been calling Matt Smith 'the boy' ever since *Confidential* unveiled him in early January 2009. It's not been a particularly well-meant nickname, but by the end of *The Eleventh Hour*, we both had to agree that the boy had done good. My mouth hit the floor, however, when I saw what they had done to the Daleks. In TV terms, it's the equivalent of defacing a monument. I hate the official line told in places like *Confidential*, where everybody stands around saying how marvellous the new design is. It's like the Emperor's new clothes – my God, hasn't anybody got eyes?!

Vincent and the Doctor, on the other hand, though unashamedly sentimental in parts, was beautifully performed by all, and *The Time of Angels* and last week's *Pandorica Opens* were exhilarating.

10.15pm (Other Stage, Pet Shop Boys) "Look," says Joe, pointing to a girl about ten places down from us. "She looks like Amy Pond."

"You wish," I said, giving him a cheeky smile. He laughed and kissed me. We laugh a lot. It's been just under two years now. He was instrumental in me coming to my first Glastonbury last year and we've done loads of things in that time.

The Pet Shop Boys set is turning out to be the best of the event so far, full of costume changes and dancers. They sing "What have I done to deserve this?" in front of a huge projection of Dusty Springfield. It's somehow incredibly moving.

"What's on this stage tomorrow night?" asks Joe. I look at 'Sunday' in my Event Guide.

"Orbital."

"Orbital are brilliant," says a bony youth behind us. "They do an amazing rave version of the *Doctor Who* theme.

Rumour is the Doctor – you know, the new one – is gonna play it with them."

"Reckon we're gonna be here then," says Joe.

"Yeah." I flash him a huge grin. "And right down the front."

If you enjoyed 'Single White Who Fan',
why not get to know Pete and Jeff...

From www.hirstpublishing.com
Turn the page for a teaser...

An Extract from 'Life Begins at 40'
By Chris Newton & Mark Charlesworth

Pete: Tuesday 22nd December

I wasn't sure what length of time spent hiding in my bedroom would be sufficient to make the point about how pissed off I was. So, after some time on the laptop – mostly spent trying top get the bloody thing to work properly – I decided it would probably be safe to re-enter the living room, just as soon as I'd done one of my 'chill out exercises', trying to name every classic Doctor Who story – in order. It was all going well until I got confused somewhere round Patrick Troughton's second season, and kept having to start from the top with 'An Unearthly Child'. Things unravelled from there, and by the time Jeff walked in, he found me in a cold sweat, repeatedly shouting "'Fury from the Deep'! 'FURY FROM THE DEEP'!!" at a wall of post-it notes.

Despite my steely determination that I would not join the others for dinner, he quickly broke down my iron resolve with the promise that he'd taken my favourite meal to new culinary heights. He wasn't wrong! I don't know if he'd switched allegiance from Heinz to Branston, but my generous serving of pasta and beans was delivered with a whole new twist. I awarded it a full 10-out-of-10 Doctors (snort!) Of course, Daisy didn't agree.

"If you boys keep tucking into those revolting, carbohydrate-saturated meals without burning off any of the calories, you'll only get fatter." She nibbled at a tiny mouthful of her 'Poulet et Arrose' and fixed Jeff with a threatening look. "I think it's about time I whip Jeffy here into shape." Giggling, she pinched his cheek. He winced.

Her guest, Tracey – who appeared from the bathroom the moment I arrived, and sat intrusively close to me – was even worse. Her bulky frame spilled out from a black cocktail dress that would have worked better as a belt. It left little to my horrified imagination, being too high to hide the crease of flesh in her buttocks, but low cut enough to show off the tattoo on her breast: a chalice toppling over and spilling its yellowy contents. I don't think it was just the glistening perspiration on her cleavage that made it look like semen. She kept looking at me and winking, licking chunks of food with her freakishly long tongue, and exaggeratedly throwing her head back as she swallowed. I think the overall effect was supposed to be sexy. I couldn't help but feel nauseous.

The meal became an increasingly tense affair and I was desperate for the girls to leave. And so it was with considerable horror that I eyed Daisy when she suggested that her and 'Jeffy' head to the bedroom to give her "astral alignment a good seeing to." I was about to adjourn to the bathroom (the only room with a lock on the door), when Daisy forced me down onto the sofa, next to Tracey.

"Ooh, this'll give you two a chance to get to know one another!" She clapped her hands together girlishly. The moment we were alone, Tracey began to advance on me. I had no idea what to do or say, so I started giving a talk about the difficulties faced by the 'Who' production team during the shift from the Second to the Third Doctor. It wasn't easy to discuss the rise of Technicolour, what with the sound of Daisy's violently enthusiastic lovemaking coming from the next room. I was also put off by the way Tracey kept inserting her index finger in and out of her mouth.

After some time, she interrupted altogether. "I'm not wearing any knickers." I had no idea why this was relevant, or how to respond, so I told her I was wearing a pair of Cybermen boxer-shorts, and went to make a cup of tea. Shortly after the kettle had boiled, Jeff walked in looking troubled, breathless, and – in a short, silk dressing-gown – remarkably camp.

"See..." He wiped his blackened eyes, frowning. "I told you everything was going to be okay."

Jeff: Wednesday 23rd December

When I finished work, all the trains were delayed because of the snow. I was stood on Platform 1 for 3 hours, in my suit, trainers and David Tennant coat, waiting for someone to comment on my outfit. No one even made eye contact.

Pete: Wednesday 23rd December

Watched last episode of 'Caves of Androzani' on repeat, and cried all day.

Jeff: Thursday 24th December

David! Please don't go! Don't leave us. It's Christmas!
I sat nibbling a mince pie and getting slowly sloshed on the Christmas beer as I leafed my way through my Doctor Who 2007 storybook. It was with teary eyes that I read the story of the little boy meeting The Doctor and Rose in a meadow, but it wasn't until I saw the illustrations of the TARDIS wrapped up beneath a Christmas tree that I broke down entirely. David! Why?

Jeff: Friday 1st January

MATT SMITH???!!!......... MATT FUCKING SMITH????

Life Begins at 40 is available from
www.hirstpublishing.com
£9.99

The author and publisher wish to thank the following people:

Brian Adams	Barnaby Eaton-Jones
Kevin Aitchison	Carl Ellis
Tristan Alfaro	Paul Engelberg
Jon Arnold	Stewart Fearon
Jamie Beckwith	Michael Gilroy-Sinclair
Jo Biza	Paul Greaves
Nicholas Blake	Ian Greenfield
Simon Bolton	Aaron Gregson
Sean Brady	Nick Griffiths
Laura Brotherton	Steve Herbert
Martin Cook	Matt Hills
Sue Cowley	Daniel Humes
Manu Das	Mark Humphrey
Steve Duerden	Simon Hunt
Will Dyson	Simon Hutchings

Linda Isele
Ruth Jenkins
Blayne Jensen
Derek Kettlety
Graham Kibble-White
Jim Lancaster
Christopher Leather
James McFetridge
Nicholas Mellish
Paul Norman
John Pettigrew
John Pettigrew
Josiah Rowe
Iain Rylands
Paul Scoones
Tim Small
Grant Smith

Paul Thomas
Robert Turner
Richard Unwin
Gary Vernon
Antony Wainer
Martin Wakefield
Stephen Walker
Alan Walsh
Lizzie Weller
Ian Wheeler
Martin Wiggins
Stephanie Wolfe
David Wright

AND:

Gary Gillatt
Tom Spilsbury
Peter Ware

More titles for Doctor Who fans from

www.hirstpublishing.com

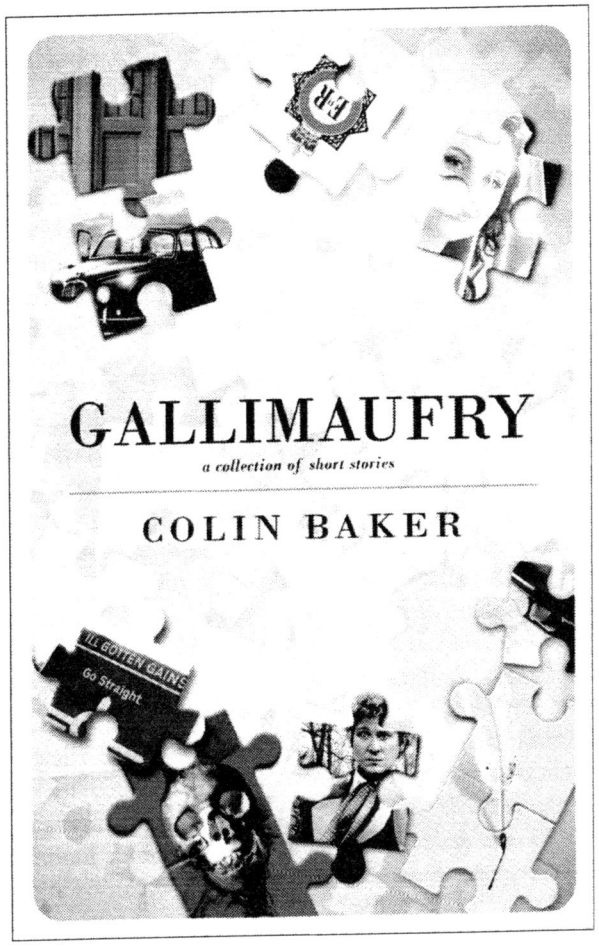

More titles for Doctor Who fans from

www.hirstpublishing.com

More titles for Doctor Who fans from

www.hirstpublishing.com

More titles for Doctor Who fans from

www.hirstpublishing.com

More titles for Doctor Who fans from

www.hirstpublishing.com

More titles for Doctor Who fans from

www.hirstpublishing.com

More titles for Doctor Who fans from

www.hirstpublishing.com

An Extract from

Flight of the Budgerigar, by John Leeson

There were occasions when K9 would be involved in scenes shot on location and although my voice would usually be added at a later stage in a dubbing theatre, I was required to join the rest of the cast and the filming crew as a matter of course. Effectively I had nothing to do other than to be there, and perhaps utter the odd line or two of K9 dialogue purely as a guide track, to be dubbed at a later stage in the sound edit. The story "The Stones of Blood" was filmed around the megalithic circle called the Rollright Stones on the Oxfordshire-Warwickshire borders, and gave rise to the already well-ventilated 'crossword' story...it is one which bears repeating here. I myself was seated in the front seat of one of the BBC's huge outside broadcast video vans about half a mile away from the actors and film crew. I had been equipped with a microphone and a pair of headphones so that my voice could be relayed to the location and I likewise could hear my cues. Through the headphones I remember hearing the director Darrol Blake calling out "take five, everyone – we're going to set up the next shot", and shortly afterwards Tom's voice came through. "Are you there, John?" he called. I confirmed I could hear him, and my voice must have come through the loudspeakers at his end of the line. "Have you got your "Times" crossword with you?" he enquired. I confirmed that I had, and we proceeded to try and crack a few clues together while the rest of the cast had been stood down. What I didn't know at the time and couldn't have seen from my distant spot was what the local villagers watching the filming from the sidelines were witnessing: Tom Baker as The Doctor sitting down on the grass verge with K9 plonked beside him, and both of them doing "The Times" crossword together! The onlookers' suspension of disbelief must have been complete!

There were two very special joys for me on that filming spree: the company of the lovely Susan Engel who played Vivien Fay, and the wonderful Beatrix Lehmann as Professor Rumford. I had asked Beatrix if she minded my taking some photographs of her on location purely for personal rather than publicity reasons, and she happily agreed. They were a great success – or at least she led me to believe so. A few days after our return to London and back into rehearsals she approached me one morning bearing a brown paper bag which she thrust into my hands. I wondered what on earth she was offering me. "This is for you, dear" she said. "I shan't be needing it again and I'd like you to have it". My amazement at opening the bag and finding a 1936 Leica camera, complete with its leather case, was overwhelming. I insisted it was far too precious a gift to give to me, let alone for a handful of black-and-white photographs I'd taken of her. "No dear" she insisted in return. "It was given to me by an old friend a long time ago – and now I want it to be yours". For my part there are times when the words 'thank you' seem poor currency in return for such a generous gift. Both Tom and I wondered if the 'old friend' might have been the actor Ralph Richardson whom she had so greatly admired and loved in her youth. Beatrix, sadly, is no longer with us. Her work on "Stones of Blood" was the last television engagement she undertook before she died. I'd like to think that she is aware… somewhere… that her camera is now safely in the custody of my film-maker son Guy who has used it to great effect for some of his own personal photographs.

Flight of the Budgerigar, by John Leeson

Published September 2011

Available to pre-order from www.hirstpublishing.com